THE J FILES
YOUTH LEADER EDITION

FOLLOW CHRIST'S EXAMPLE

By Calvin Miller
and
Jane Wilson Brinkley

Copyright © 1997 • Convention Press
All Rights Reserved
5130-48

This book is a resource in the Christian Growth Study Plan.

ISBN: 0–7673–2964–3
Dewey Decimal Classification number: 248.84
Subject Heading: Spiritual Life\Jesus Christ—
Public Ministry

Printed in the United States of America
Available from Customer Service Center
1–800–458–2772 and Baptist Book Stores

Ministry Design and Resources Section
Ministry and Leadership Development
Department
Bible Teaching-Reaching Division
The Sunday School Board of the Southern Baptist
Convention
127 Ninth Avenue, North
Nashville, Tennessee 37234-0177

Acknowledgements:
Unless otherwise notes, Scripture quotations are from the Holy Bible, *New International Version* © copyright 1973, 1978, 1984 by International Bible Society.

Table of contents

chapter 1
Follow Me — 6

chapter 2
Pray With Me — 24

chapter 3
Love One Another — 42

chapter 4
Love Your Neighbor — 60

chapter 5
I Am Sending You — 78

FOREWORD

"Follow me," He said. And they did—fishermen and tax collectors, religious leaders and prostitutes, scholars and demoniacs, rich and poor, the diseased, disabled, disowned, and despised men and women, youth and children—as many as would receive Him. Jesus Christ called His followers from the darkness of a world that had lost its way and gave them Himself to carry back into that world. Nothing has been the same since. Christ is calling us to continue the ministry He gave to those first disciples. Are you ready to do that as a teenager or a leader with youth?

Following Christ requires sacrifice. We must be willing to lay aside our own lives for the good of others. Jesus did. We must be people of prayer, bringing to God our concerns for our own lives, for other Christians, and for those who do not know Christ. Jesus did this as well. To be effective, youth and youth leaders must love one another as Christ loved us. We are to lift up, encourage, and serve one another and the youth entrusted to our care as Christ did His disciples. We are to love our neighbors as ourselves, reaching out to those who are different from us, loving them, seeking to meet their needs, offering them friendship, sharing with them the wonderful news of salvation. Jesus did all these things, and Christ's ministry expanded through His followers. Just as the Father sent Christ into the world to redeem it through His sacrifice, Jesus sent His disciples to do the same.

As you study this book, I believe you will be inspired to follow Christ's example. Calvin Miller uses his own unique storytelling style to bring to life five episodes from Christ's life and ministry as Simon Peter might have experienced them. Jane Wilson Brinkley has followed each of those "J Files" with contemporary examples of how today's Youth Sunday School classes, departments, and other groups might respond to the example of Christ, extending His ministry in ways that are practical and effective in meeting the real needs of today's teenagers. Here is an opportunity to learn how to teach teens to pray and to build unity through prayer; to lead youth to develop servant attitudes; to help youth develop practical strategies for extending the love, witness, and fellowship of Christ to others regardless of their background; and to call youth into service as new leaders themselves. Jesus is calling,"Follow me!" The next step is ours.

Bill Taylor, Director
Bible Teaching-Reaching Division
The Sunday School Board
of the Southern Baptist Convention

ABOUT THE WRITERS

Calvin Miller is Professor of Communication and Ministry Studies and Writer in Residence at Southwestern Baptist Theological Seminary, Ft. Worth, Texas, where he has served since November, 1991. He is a graduate of Oklahoma Baptist University and Midwestern Baptist Theological Seminary. He has written or contributed to a great number of books and publications, and been guest lecturer at several colleges, universities, and seminaries. Miller is a native of Oklahoma.

Jane Wilson Brinkley, the writer of the youth portion of *The J Files*, is an experienced writer of all types of Youth Sunday School materials.

She is a graduate of Baylor University, with a Master of Science in Education and she earned a Master's of Religious Education degree from Southwestern Baptist Theological Seminary.

Jane is a former youth minister and director of a Youth Sunday School High School Department at North Fort Worth Baptist Church. She is a popular youth conference leader for the Baptist General Convention of Texas. Jane and her husband Mike are residents of Fort Worth.

chapter 1

Follow Me

It was in the eighteenth year of Tiberius that I looked for the last time to the Sea of Tiberias for my income. I hated calling it the Sea of Tiberias. It was Galilee to me—the Sea of Galilee—and we who fished on it called it by its proper name. Galilee had been given this name in honor of the Emperor Tiberius. The Gentile emperors were all cases of strutting ego, ever naming this and that after themselves. Whatever one called it, the sea was good fishing—sometimes. And it was pretty—sometimes. And when it wasn't good fishing, it was bad, and when it wasn't pretty, it could be just plain violent.

Overall, Galilee is the most difficult pond of water in the world. I had a love/hate affair with that sometimes little, sometimes big, lake. Thirty years I had spent lugging nets, throwing the soggy cords, digging out the trash carp and saving the good fish.

My brother Andrew had always helped me. But in the fifteenth year of Tiberius, he got religion. I mean really serious religion. Andrew was quiet, most of the time. He was a sincere man, but he had always shown a little too much reverence for itinerant preachers to suit me. Furthermore, Andrew had always prayed a little too much. I don't necessarily mind a person praying, but when there's work to be done, there's work to be done. And it seemed to me Andrew sometimes prayed when he should have been fishing.

I had spoken to him several times about the fact that we were still partners in a fishing business, and it sure would be nice if he could help do a little more of the fishing. Each time I got on him he'd get better for a little while. But then he'd slip back into his old habits and sneak off to hear some itinerant faith healer. It made me as mad as a cobra staring down a mongoose.

Like I said, in the fifteenth year of Tiberius Andrew became infatuated with John the Baptist, a new prophet from south of Galilee who was preaching that the Messiah was coming. The message wasn't all that unusual—everyone was preaching that some messiah was coming.

Messianic prophets were generally not all that unusual; John was uncommonly unusual. He preached a little louder than I thought necessary and he dressed in animal skins. I asked Andrew why it was that this "wild man from Jordan" didn't turn him off.

"Look Andrew, the guy is weird," I shouted. "Stay away from him!"

"I don't think he's so weird."

"You think wearing animal skins is normal?"

"Well," said Andrew, "Elijah lived down there in those jungles a thousand years ago and he wore animal skins. It's just a prophet's way of rejecting modern culture. John doesn't even go shopping in open markets. He detests them."

"Well, what does he eat?"

"You don't want to know," replied Andrew.

I found out later what he ate. It was enough to turn my stomach. But that's how a lot of these kingdom preachers were—weird. Some of these preachers even set dates for the end of the world. Some of them, like the Zealots, were extremists, buying dried goods and contraband weapons so that when the big and final war came they would be ready.

Neither Andrew nor I liked the Romans, but we had already decided we weren't going to join the Zealots. Still, once Andrew met this strange, kingdom preacher out in the wilderness, he lost all interest in fishing. (He didn't have much interest to begin with, it seemed to me.)

One day, when I was all but fed up with Andrew's loss of interest in fishing, he came running in and said, "I've seen the Messiah!"

"Who's the man of the hour this time, Andrew?" I was totally upset.

"Please Simon, come with me," Andrew begged.

"If I do will you get back to work? Do I need to remind you it's time to retar the boats and replace some of the nets? It's been a bad month. We're not making all that much money anymore."

"OK, OK." He grinned. "But first come and see the Messiah named Jesus. Then I'll come back to work."

Well, I went with him. I must be honest, I was all set to be unimpressed. There were about three new messiahs through town every month in those days. All of them found someone like Andrew, gullible enough to follow them and give them the last of the family fortune. Andrew, God bless him, loved God, and it was hard for me not to respect that. But I felt good that one of us—namely me—had the good common sense to keep working so that the other—namely Andrew—could walk around agog at the latest one who claimed the messianic title.

Then I saw Jesus.

It wasn't a large crowd that He stood before, but it was an ardent group. Jesus just stood there, talking quietly. No loud theatrical lectures. No wide sweeping, vainglorious gestures. Just a man so pure of heart that you could almost feel His goodness.

I could see why Andrew was so taken with the man. I felt the same way.

When the lecture was over, I walked up to Jesus. I thought I would say something nice, like I sometimes said to the rabbi on the way out of the synagogue. But before I could say anything, He caught my sleeve and said to me, "You're Simon the son of John, aren't you?" It was unnerving. Obviously Andrew had told Him my name—or had he? I had this odd feeling that He knew me before Andrew had told Him a lot about our family.

When He told me my name, well, I stammered. I was supposed to tell Him my name; that's the way introductions work. Then He said the oddest thing. "From now on, your name is going to be Cephas." Now is that weird or what? I really hadn't gone to Jesus to be renamed. I was just out to meet Andrew's new religious friends.

I started to protest the name when I looked into Jesus' eyes. It was like looking into the middle of forever! It was like He was God enough to name anybody anything He wanted to. I felt such an odd sensation of fear and wonder. I couldn't get my mouth dry enough to say anything. Besides, the power of His look said it was better not to say anything—which was unusual for me.

Well, for the rest of the day, I didn't say anything. However that night, when we were settling down for bed, I asked Andrew, "What kind of new name did He give you today?"

"Nothing. I'm still Andrew. But if He gave you a new name, you can be sure that He's got His eye on you for something special."

"Oh yeah! Well, I like Simon bar-Jona pretty good. If I wanted a new name, I'd get me a lawyer and . . . ."

"Good night, Cephas!" Andrew smiled, looking at me oddly, and blew out the lamp.

I decided to stay around another day. Who knows? I thought. Maybe I'll pick up a new middle name, too.

On the next day, Jesus announced that He was headed back to Galilee. As He started out, with all of us following behind, He saw a man named Philip of Bethsaida. Philip had Andrew's reputation for running off in search of every new field preacher. So, I don't know that I was all that surprised at what happened next.

"Follow Me!" Jesus said to Philip.

Philip did. Just like that. Just like Andrew had. Then Philip did a most erratic thing. He said, "I'll be right back. I've got to go tell my brother!

Poor brother, I thought to myself. I wonder if he'll get renamed too? What was this odd power Jesus had? How was it that He affected all of us? Why was everyone so eager to quit a good job and wander around listening to sermons out in the fields?

Philip was back in a short time, dragging his brother with him. He brought him right up to Jesus. Jesus reached past Philip and took the man's shoulders in His hands. He said aloud, as though He was speaking to the whole world at once, "Behold, an Israelite who is incapable of evil thinking."

Nathanael (that was Philip's brother's name—his real name, I think) was a little baffled at the statement. "Do you know me?" he asked.

Jesus smiled and nodded, "Before Philip called you, while you were under the fig tree, I saw you."

It was all so very cryptic. What was Nathanael doing under the fig tree? What was he thinking? When Jesus said He saw him there, He seemed to be talking of more things than could be seen with the eyes. He seemed to indicate He had caught Nathanael in some kind of reverie, perhaps musing over who Jesus really was or whether he should accept all His claims as Philip had. Whatever mental state he was in while under the fig tree, Jesus must have caught him red-handed in these meanderings of the heart. Nathanael blurted out, "You are the Son of God, the King of Israel."

Now that statement all by itself made me want to know more about Jesus. But as much as Nathanael's greeting overwhelmed my mind, I could not imagine why Jesus did not rebuke Nathanael for such impropriety. Why would anybody let someone else refer to him as the Son of God and the King of Israel—unless he really was?

I soon grew tired of trying to sort through the bold claims of this Jesus. He was a man or a messiah that I really didn't want to believe in anyway. I needed some time to separate from the whole scene. I left Jesus and went on back to Galilee. Andrew came with me.

Andrew had always been good about giving me the space I needed to ferret out the things I needed to decide. Was Jesus the Messiah or not? Was Andrew right or wrong? Should I follow or not? How would I keep my family alive if I quit fishing? Was it reasonable to expect God to take care of them while I was off acting like Andrew, chasing messiahs and pursuing Israel's hope? My thoughts turned in on themselves. I wanted to believe, but, oh, the cost of giving up everything for the sake of a man whom I really didn't know all that well.

At last we were home. Ah Galilee! How often through life I had turned to the sea to help me sort through what I was unable to understand on dry land. I spent a lot of "boat time" as Andrew called it; the questions still filled my mind. Was Jesus the Messiah? Should I accept my new name and give up fishing to follow Him? I was a troubled man. I fished and thought and thought and fished.

Andrew and I had been back at Galilee only for a week or so. Early one morning, before we had set out to sea, we were doing some net casting along the shore. There He came to us. Jesus was there in person! He walked up, looked at Andrew, and then He turned His head my way. His eyes, burning like a star-beam afire, pierced my defenses. It seemed He was looking right down into my turbulent soul. Our vision locked eye-to-eye. He said, "Follow Me, and I will make you a fisher of men!"

Next to being named Cephas, it was one of the most unusual moments I have ever experienced. I knew exactly what I was doing that morning when I walked off the job. Somehow Andrew knew too. But why? Why would two men walk away from a life handed down by their father who was a fisherman before them? There was only one answer. Jesus had spoken! He said, "Follow Me," and we did.

I'm not saying I've always made good rational decisions, but when Jesus said, "Follow Me," I became as irresponsible as I had always accused Andrew of being. The difference was I had a family.

But I was genuinely learning, not just about Scriptures but about life. I was spellbound by Jesus' teachings and awed by His miracles. However, it may have been Matthew's call that helped me understand the power of those words "Follow Me." For soon after I left Galilee, Jesus, and those of us who were following Him, passed by this tax collector named Matthew. I had my opinions about tax collectors, just like I did about many other things and people. I was all in favor of Jesus saying "Follow Me" to whomever He wanted. And, I think that when Jesus says "Follow Me," a person is under some obligation to do it.

But to be truthful, when He said "Follow Me" to Matthew, I was hoping Matthew would say, "No deal! I'm a Jewish financial leech after Roman payola. I can't afford to become an itinerant evangelist; I'm not good at self-denial. I like gouging the system and watching the sestertius fall into my bag. Nope! No deal, Jesus! I'm not following!"

Imagine the horror the rest of us felt when Matthew said in crisp Aramaic, "Yes, Jesus. I will follow You!" He got up right then from his tax-stand. He even invited us all to a big dinner at his house. Jesus accepted for us all.

We all went to Matthew's house for dinner. We disciples traveled around a lot, sleeping outside and eating a lot of old fish. So we were always ready for a good meal. But I wasn't sure I was ready for Matthew's spread. These publicans were rich, living off the money they stole from their fellow Jews. Many, like Matthew, built villas. Etiquette in social situations was not easy for some of us. Take our treasurer, for instance—Judas was from Kerioth. He felt that eating utensils were slower than fingers and cuffs worked better than napkins. I'm not sure any of us fit into the posh surroundings of this publican's feast.

Some of the Pharisees were there and they severely criticized Jesus' choice of followers. "Down to publicans for disciples, are we?" they taunted. I was grateful they didn't mention fishermen. Still, it seemed a fair question.

Matthew was the son of Alphaeus. He had a brother whom Jesus had also called to be a disciple: James bar-Alphaeus. I always wondered how James must have felt about his "Roman sellout" of a brother. James may have been unhappy that Jesus had called out to Matthew. He may have been even more unhappy than the rest of us that Matthew had followed. We were a strange mix of disciples. But here we all were reclining for dinner at Matthew's house.

Secretly most of us pretty well agreed with the Pharisees. If we hadn't been so hungry and if the dinner hadn't been such a feast, we might have walked out. Matthew's cook made these little square honey cakes that were served with whole cream, and well—it sure gets hard to argue with the sins of rich people when they're feeding you so good.

Anyway, one of the Pharisees said in a kind of stage whisper but loud enough for all of us to hear, "Why is Jesus eating with Matthew, the publican and sinner?"

Sinner is a harsh word, but let's face it—Matthew was a sinner; all publicans were sinners. Pharisees sinned a little but not enough for most folks to keep track of. We fishermen sinned a little more. While we could keep track of our sins, even our sins were nothing in comparison to publicans. Those guys were sinners—big time. Plus they were rich sinners, and rich sinners are hard for poor sinners to forgive.

Anyway, once the Pharisees were through criticizing Jesus for choosing Matthew, it was Jesus' response that really made us mad. He said, "They that are sick need a physician, not those who are well." I agreed—partly. Matthew was a Roman-tax-collecting-price-gouging sicko. But was Jesus implying that the Pharisees were well and healthy, and we disciples were sinners? Somehow the honey cakes and fresh cream didn't taste so good anymore. I quit after two.

I would have considered Jesus' "Follow Me" to Matthew a complete waste, except the next morning when we were ready to leave Matthew's house, Matthew was all packed. He had his own little ruck-sack laying by his huge cedar doors. He was going with us. What was more unusual was that when I got up, he was having a little cup of milk with James, his brother. Apparently Matthew was taking Jesus' "Follow Me" seriously. Matthew and James were laughing together.

Matthew left with us. Just like that, he left his tax business, just like I had walked away from my fishing business. He walked around with us and followed Jesus from place to place. And what an odd collection we were: fishermen, publicans, Zealots, and general all-around revivalists. I wasn't sure I liked thinking about my self-image as a part of this group.

A couple of days later, I discovered we were all headed back into Galilee. When we got back to our house, I learned my mother-in-law was sick, bad sick.

My wife was almost out of her mind with fear. Her mother's temperature was dangerously high, and not one of the physicians in Capernaum had been able to break it. In all our years of marriage, we had never faced the kind of crisis that left us staring death in the face. Jesus seemed to know our fear. I hadn't known Him long, but I perceived a certain look on His face, a look I would see many times in the days to come.

That look. It always happened the same way: His eyes got moist, like something inside Him was crying. Jesus was moved inwardly by any pain that gripped and destroyed those about Him. After the moist eyes, you could see Jesus get rigid, as though He was steeling Himself to fight some unseen enemy. Then, like a warrior going into battle, He would walk confidently toward the suffering one.

That is how He walked toward the bed on which my mother-in-law was lying. He took her by the hand and rebuked her fever. Then He smiled. She smiled back. I laughed at the pure release of the weight of the strain that had fallen off my family. Joy was everywhere!

My mother-in-law is an untiring hostess. She was no sooner healthy again than she looked about, as I had seen her do many times, looking for what needed to be done. "Oh my goodness!" she gasped. "You must all be starving." She began to serve us. I couldn't help but weep.

Why the emotion? I saw the healed serving her Healer. Why? Because in some way other than direct words, Jesus had said to my mother-in-law, "Follow Me!" She got off her sick bed at His words. Immediately she felt the need to serve Him and others. There must have been an ongoing "Follow Me" in her life just like in mine. If you were going to follow, you had to do what Jesus said, even if you were dying when He said it. Service and servanthood became a priority.

"Follow Me." None dare disobey the imperative. We all had heard the words, and none of us would ever be the same again. No words of Jesus would change as many lives and fortunes, as many dreams and destinies, as those two glorious words: Follow Me! Andrew was changed by those words. So were Philip and Nathanael. And don't forget the sons of Zebedee. So were Matthew and his brother James. I, too, followed. We followed because we had no choice. We followed because we were compelled by love—His love for us, our love for Him.

As I see it, when Jesus says "Follow Me" you either do or you don't. If you don't, you are a fool. If you do, well, then you become part of two worlds: the world at hand and the one on the way.

Follow Me!

Have you ever accepted an invitation to go on an excursion when you weren't quite sure where you were going or what it would involve? To an adult, such an event may not be too common. But, to teenagers, it is not at all unusual! Such was the experience of Matthew when he accepted Jesus' invitation spoken in two words: "Follow Me." That invitation undoubtedly proved to be far more dramatic, consuming, and life-changing than Matthew ever imagined. Yes, Jesus asked Matthew (a tax collector!) to follow Him, and Matthew did. And Christ has been asking people to follow Him since that day.

This call may mean the actual loss of physical life, or the death of one's previously well-thought-out plans and dreams—but it is death. The words, *Follow Me* comprise an open-ended invitation. We do not know where the words will lead us—we know only that we must die in some way to fulfill them. We must pay a price. Between the words *Follow Me* and meeting Christ face-to-face lies a lifetime of obedience.

Following Christ means being prepared to take risks. There must be no competition in the area of loyalties. One must say *yes* to God and *no* to self in the same way Adam said *no* to God and *yes* to self.

Why would a person choose such a life of following Christ? A junior high student discussed her interest in becoming a Christian with her unbelieving mother. The mother replied, "Why would you want to be anyone's slave?" The Christian life may often appear to be quite a difficult and burdensome lifestyle. Yet, if we choose to give up the yoke Christ lays upon us—the one He made specifically for us—we find we have a much heavier burden to bear: the yoke of our own choosing, the yoke of ourselves. As Christ clearly said in Matthew 11:29-30: *Take my yoke upon you, and learn from me; for I am gentle and lowly in heart, and you will find rest for your souls. For my yoke is easy and my burden is light.*[1] When we willingly submit to the call of Christ, He affirms our own uniqueness and gifts. We discover purpose and ministry among others. It may not initially be the easiest path, but it is undoubtedly the most rewarding. After all, God created us and we can trust Him to know what will bring us fulfillment and make us useful for His kingdom. We truly are fools to say *no*!

The apostle Paul desired the greatest possible identification with his Savior, Jesus Christ. Being "crucified with Christ" is how he described it in Galatians 2:20: *With Christ I stand crucified* may be the better translation of the word order and perfect tense. Stated either way, it is a powerful statement of Paul's commitment to his Lord. In Philippians 3:10 he makes the dramatic statement of his desire not only to know the power of Christ's resurrection, but to share in his sufferings. Why would anyone wish for such a thing? Paul understood there are two sides to the knowledge of Christ: A disciple must share in the sufferings as well as the power. We don't relate to suffering and will probably never know the real depth of such a request as the one Paul made. But, it is a part of accepting the awesome and seemingly mysterious invitation, *Follow Me*.

Write your own idea of what is involved in following Jesus. What parts of identity with Christ do you eagerly accept? What parts do you often avoid?

You may be saying to yourself right now, This writer is taking the whole idea of being a follower of Christ just a little too far! Let's give more thought and study to the whole meaning of Christ's invitation. Mark 2:14 states: *As he walked along, he saw Levi son of Alphaeus sitting at the tax collector's booth. 'Follow me,' Jesus told him, and Levi got up and followed him.* The word *followed* clearly denotes a relationship of disciple to teacher. This call to commitment is relational rather than intellectual or emotional. At the center of the call is a person, not an idea or a task. Such a personal invitation may be threatening to many of us—we'd rather have a contract that clearly spells out and limits our obligations. We are uncomfortable agreeing to something so open-ended; something so dynamic and changeable that depends upon a relationship with someone. But, that's how Christ established His whole idea of discipleship, or following Him. He obviously knew it would work better for everyone that way.

Upon landing at Vera Cruz in 1519 with 700 men to begin his conquest of Mexico, Cortez intentionally set fire to his fleet of 11 ships. His soldiers watched as their only means of departure was consumed in flames and sank to the bottom of the Gulf of Mexico. Cortez knew that, with no means of retreat, there was only one direction to go: forward into Mexico to take over the land. As we decide to follow Christ, we, too, must get rid of everything that might enable us to retreat.[2]

The Bible gives us insight through the words of Christ Himself. One of Jesus' clearest statements is found in Luke 9:23-24: *Then He said to them all, 'If anyone chooses to be my disciple, he must say No to self, put the cross on his shoulders daily, and continue to follow me. For whoever chooses to save his lower life will lose his higher life, but whoever gives up his lower life for my sake will save his higher life.'*[3]

The Greek word *mathethes (disciple)* signifies a learner or apprentice. This may be an adequate definition for a disciple of a rabbi or Greek philosopher, but it falls very short of describing a disciple of Christ.

Examine some of the conditions for following Jesus. Underline the aspects of each condition of discipleship that are most difficult for you.

- *Say no to self.*—I must place my hope in God's plan for my future. Am I willing to give up my claim to my life, surrender my personal ambitions, and abandon myself to Christ?

- *Put the cross on your shoulders daily.*—The cross is not only the instrument of Christ's death, but the instrument through which I offer myself to God's will instead of my own. Am I willing to endure anything because of my loyalty to Him?

- *Continue to follow Him.*—The verb tense tells us that following Christ is a continuous action. We must not give up; we must not quit, even when we grow weary. Do I have this type of endurance?

Are you ready to follow in the fullness of a deeper understanding of what following really requires? What would Jesus say to you as you consider such an important step? Take a look at what Jesus said to those who expressed interest in following Him:

- *Anyone who loves his father or mother more than me is not worthy of me; anyone who loves his son or daughter more than me is not worthy of me; and anyone who does not take his cross and follow me is not worthy of me* (Matt. 10:37-38). Jesus was not condoning disobedience or disrespect toward parents, or neglect of children; but He was reminding the disciples of what must be their first priority.

- *Jesus looked at [the young man] and loved him. One thing you lack, he said. Go, sell everything you have and give to the poor, and you will have treasure in heaven. Then come, follow me* (Mark 10:21). This young man's love of money prevented his total commitment to Christ. The Bible tells us that he went away from Christ with sadness, for he wasn't willing to give all he had for Christ's kingdom.

- *Let the dead bury their own dead, but you go and proclaim the kingdom of God*

(Luke 9:60). When Jesus was on the road to Jerusalem, a man asked if he could bury his father before following Him. We do not know if the father had actually died or if the man wanted to delay following until after the father was dead. Jesus was not encouraging the neglect of family responsibilities, but He wanted the man to stop using his father as an excuse to delay following Him.

• *Jesus replied, 'No one who puts his hand to the plow and looks back is fit for service in the kingdom of God'* (Luke 9:62). On the same occasion as the previous example He told a potential follower there was no time for him to say good-bye to his family. These words seem severe, but Jesus was emphasizing the need for abandoning everything to follow Him. One must be willing to cut ties to the past. A person cannot plow forward in a straight line while looking back over his shoulder.

Do you have a situation similar to any of these? What or who is holding you back from a 100 per cent total commitment to following Christ? What things in your life interfere with your following Him? List them in the space below. Try to see your life as you think Christ sees it.

The person who accepts the call of Christ is a disciple, or learner. The Bible tells us much about the life of a disciple. Review these descriptions of a disciple. Place an *x* on the line that marks where you evaluate your likeness to each statement, with *0* being not like you at all and *10* being very much like you.

1. A disciple seeks to glorify God in all he does.
   0_____5_____10

2. A disciple has an active and growing prayer life.
   0_____5_____10

3. A disciple forgives others.
   0_____5_____10

4. A disciple worships with other believers.
   0_____5_____10

5. A disciple gives of his resources generously and privately.
   0_____5_____10

6. A disciple is prepared to share his testimony for Christ.
   0_____5_____10

7. A disciple goes where people need Christ .
   0_____5_____10

8. A disciple is a servant.
   0_____5_____10

9. A disciple studies the Word of God.
   0_____5_____10

10. A disciple shows the fruits of the Holy Spirit.
    0_____5_____10

11. A disciple is willing to examine his or her life.
    0_____5_____10

12. A disciple does everything in love.
    0_____5_____10

13. A disciple seeks to live a pure life.
    0_____5_____10

14. A disciple puts Christ first.
    0_____5_____10

15. A disciple is ready for Christ's return.
    0_____5_____10

Which of the fifteen characteristics listed above is most descriptive of you? Which is least descriptive of you? Write a statement of what God might want you to do to strengthen your weakest areas.

_____

Why is submission to Christ difficult for so many of us? It appears we are in a constant battle of the will. We present Christ with our many excuses, often refusing to honestly face why we won't yield our lives to His control. If, however, we trust God to save us from an eternity of separation from Him, why can't we trust Him in our everyday lives? Here are a few possibilities:

1. We believe we know what is best for us. This may be the heart of our resistance—expressed in ten words or less. Instead of viewing ourselves as the creation and God as the creator and the one who knows us best, we try to be our own god. We place our knowledge of our well-being above His knowledge of us.

2. We think God may not really have our best interests at heart. We may miss out on something good by allowing Him this type of control. (The God who gave everything He had to restore fellowship with us isn't looking out for us?) When we honestly face our feelings here, the error of our thinking becomes obvious.

3. God may ask us to do something we don't want to do. There is an element of truth in this statement, for we will not initially want to do everything God requires of us.

4. What I give to God may be taken away from me completely. Can we not trust God to wisely use what we give to Him? Is it possible to give Him something we need and Him refuse to return it to us for our use? This is another example of reasoning which is in direct opposition to scripture.

5. He may ask me to do something I am physically or emotionally unable to do. (This is an impossibility in God's economy. It will never happen. You may not have the strength on your own, but God will give you what you need to accomplish His will.)

6. He may alter the goals I have set for my life and that of my family. Quite frankly, many of us can count on this one to be true! For many, our goals and desires before yielding to Christ prove to be inadequate as we follow Him. We must listen carefully as He reveals His plan for our lives, trusting it to be the best.

Teens may offer these excuses for not yielding their lives to Christ:

- He may not allow me to get married! (usually the girls!)

- He may make me marry someone I don't want to marry! (usually the boys!)

- Following Him is not as much fun as not following Him.

- I want to make a lot of money when I grow up; following Him may interfere with that goal.

- I don't want to seem like a freak or weird person; I want to be "normal".

Over a period of several years, teenagers gave the following responses when asked what changes would be necessary in their lives if they followed Christ in the way He desires. You probably will not be surprised at the responses, the majority of which may be summarized in nine statements:

1. My attitude would have to change.

2. My relationship with my parents would have to be different.

3. I would have to stop using alcohol.

4. I would have to spend more time with God—in His Word and in prayer.

5. I would have to change the way I talk.

6. I would have to change the way I behave around others.

7. My need for the approval of others would have to lessen.

8. I would have to become a Christian.

9. I would have to allow a "total overhaul" of my life.

Many of the core issues of life are the same for people of all ages. Let's translate these nine issues from those youth might face to issues that pertain more specifically to adults. Carefully consider the questions that follow each issue.

1. Attitude: Do I have bad attitudes toward others? Toward some of my responsibilities? About what God is asking me to be or do? Do I hold God responsible for everything that is happening in my life today?

2. Relationship with parents, which translates in two areas for adults. Authority issues: Do I have difficulty with authority? Is my relationship with Christ evident in the way I deal with my employer? With legal authorities? Family issues: Do I neglect my family to pursue business or social interests? Do my actions show my work to be more important to me than my family relationships?

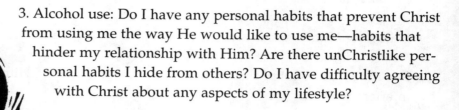

3. Alcohol use: Do I have any personal habits that prevent Christ from using me the way He would like to use me—habits that hinder my relationship with Him? Are there unChristlike personal habits I hide from others? Do I have difficulty agreeing with Christ about any aspects of my lifestyle?

4. Time alone with God: Is time in the Word and in prayer a daily priority? Is anything else on my morning agenda more important than meeting God for a few minutes before I begin my day? Do I feel I can make it on my own each day and wait to call on Him when I run into trouble?

5. The spoken word: Do I use God's name carelessly or in vain? Do I use vulgar or profane language? Do I build others up or tear them down? Would I be embarrassed for others to read a transcript of the words I have spoken during the past 24 hours?

6. Change actions around others: Do I act one way around Christians and another way around my friends who do not know the Lord? Am I hesitant to stand up for my Christian beliefs or share a positive word about my relationship with the Lord?

7. Too much emphasis on the approval of others: Am I more concerned with what others think than what God thinks? For whose "well done" am I striving?

8. Accept Christ as Savior: Do I know Christ in a personal way or do I simply know *about* Him? (There is an eternal difference between these two concepts.)

9. The need for a "total overhaul:" Have I been directing my life and not yielding control to Him? Is it time to stop "playing" at following Christ?

Many changes were necessary for Brantley Smith when he decided to follow the call of Christ for his life. Now a music student at Southwestern Baptist Theological Seminary in Ft. Worth, Texas, Smith helped to create the rock band "Hootie and the Blowfish" in 1985 while a student at the University of South Carolina. By 1989 the band had developed a regional rock band "Hootie and the Blowfish" in 1985 while a student at the University of South Carolina. By 1989 the band had developed a regional following, but Smith felt God had different plans for his life. He felt he was not doing all he could do with the ability God had given him. He made the decision to leave the band and begin studying to become a minister of music. Though it is reported that the members of the rock band earn $60,000 a week, Smith says he does not regret his decision at all, stating, "It was fun to be part of a band that has a growing popularity, but it is more of a joy to be where God wants me to be."[4]

One of the most exciting aspects of living the Christian life in relationship with other believers is observing how they live out Christ's invitation, *Follow Me*. For God, it must be terribly disappointing at times to see how minimally (and how seldom) we assess our actions in this life of following Him. We don't seem to understand the importance of a vital, living relationship with the One we follow. Remember, it is the relationship that governs what we do. We are not ruled by a creed, contract, or set of laws.

Do you sometimes have difficulty defining your life as a disciple? Maturity in age is not always the determining factor to finding answers to the question of how one lives out the invitation of Christ. Consider these examples of young men and women who have demonstrated a very clear idea of what Jesus' *Follow Me* means in their lives.

• Danny Wuerffel, senior quarterback at the University of Florida, turned down the "Scholar Athlete Award" for Playboy magazine's 1996 preseason college All-America football team. He stated, "It's just not something I want to be associated with, and there are a whole lot of bad connotations that go along with that magazine."[5] Wuerffel is a popular speaker at True Love Waits rallies and youth conferences sponsored by the Florida Baptist Convention.

• Charity Allen, while a student at the Los Angeles High School for the Performing Arts, was offered a role in the soap opera "Another World." It was a lucrative contract—including private tutoring, chauffeured limos, a townhouse in New York City for her entire family, and a salary of up to $20,000 a week. When she learned her character was to have an affair with a married man, engage in a bedroom scene with the lead singer of a rock band, and eventually become pregnant, she turned down the role. "There's no way I can ever be a part of that. That's betraying everything I believe in."[6]

These two examples may appear to be somewhat unbelievable because they involve giving up two of the major enticements of our world today: athletic recognition and movie/television fame. What most of the world would view as wonderful opportunities were viewed by these two young Christians as inappropriate for someone who has answered Christ's invitation to follow Him. There are countless other teenagers who are not faced with such high-profile and glamorous decisions, but who make choices that are just as important. There is the high school student whose recently-divorced mother entered her room one summer morning the week before the school year began, saying "We are moving to Texas today. Get your things packed." This young disciple had made a decision at youth camp that summer to follow Christ to the mission field. She states, "I dealt with this unexpected move by viewing it as part of my first mission assignment." Her personal translation of *Follow Me* turned a very dark time in her life into an occasion to seek the guiding hand of God.[7]

Consider, also, the teenager who, after a youth mission trip to an inner-city area, decided that she would no longer wear designer clothes. Those clothes did not fit into her personal walk with Christ.

There are still other teenagers who take Christ's directive with utmost seriousness as they choose not to cheat in school, have premarital sex, or abuse their bodies with alcohol and drugs. Eighteen-year-old Summer Newman, Alabama's 1996 Junior Miss, states, "God has blessed me in so many ways, and He has a plan for my life. I don't want to hinder that by having sex before marriage." Teens like Summer are making decisions many adults have great difficulty making. They are defining the challenges and privileges of discipleship, growing daily in their "following" skills as they grow in their personal relationship with Christ. Of course, there are adults, too, who make difficult choices each day as they file accurate and honest income tax returns, refuse to give in to temptations of extramarital sexual activity, and refrain from lying as a matter of convenience, seeking in their part of life to walk in a manner consistent with their understanding of Jesus' *Follow Me*.

One of the clearest statements of discipleship captures the meaning of those words in a precise way: Whoever claims to live in Him must walk as Jesus did. The fullest expression of a relationship with Christ is obedience to Him and imitation of Him. My answer to His invitation to follow must be made with my life. The challenge is extraordinary, and clear—I must do what Jesus would do.

Follow Me! These words open and close many doors of experience in the life of one who follows. Where could such a life of discipleship eventually lead? Only God Himself knows. No one else can predict what lies ahead after you've decided to follow. But, there is only one answer to Christ's invitation for the person who wants the truly abundant life—YES!

stretching

How is God leading me to leave my comfort zone and deepen my response to Jesus' invitation, *Follow Me*?

1. Scripture quotations Marked (NIV) Holy Bible, *New International Version*. Copyright @ 1973, 1978, 1984 by International Bible Society.
2. Walter Henrichsen, *Disciples are Made — Not Born* (Wheaton, Ill.: Victor Books, 1974), 40.
3. *Williams New Testament* (Chicago: IL, 1952)
4. *The Baptist Standard*, Oct. 16, 1996, 11.
5. *The Baptist Standard*, Vol. 108, No. 21, May 22, 1996.
6. *Living With Teenagers*, May, 1996.
7. *Living With Teenagers*, Oct., 1996.

chapter 2

Pray With Me

The greatest lesson I learned from Jesus on prayer caused me a great deal of pain. It happened on Thursday. We had the Passover meal in the upper room of John Mark's house. It was pretty late when we left there and went out to Olive Press Park where we often camped. Jesus preferred that campsite because it was quiet. We could sleep pretty soundly there.

That particular Thursday night we were really tired. So we were all a little eager to get to sleep. It was late when we got to Gethsemane, and the day had been crammed with pre-Passover expectations.

For some reason Jesus wanted to spend some late-night time in prayer. That was not all that unusual, but that night Jesus wanted company. He wanted some of us to go and pray with Him because He said He was extremely sorrowful. So James, John and I went with Him and left the others under the olive trees. Jesus asked us to pray nearby in our part of the park while He went on farther.

I wasn't much in the mood for praying—I was dead tired. I was sure we had walked a hundred miles that day! Well, anyway, Jesus went out there and started to pray. I heard Him praying:

Father, the time has come. Glorify your Son, that your Son may glorify you. For you granted him authority over all people that he might give eternal life to all those you have given him. Now this is eternal life: that they may know you, the only true God, and Jesus Christ, whom you have sent. I have brought you glory on earth by completing the work you gave me to do. And now, Father, glorify me and in your presence with the glory I had with you before the world began (John 17:1-5, NIV).

I was nodding off. I couldn't think straight. I wondered what He meant by that word *glorify*. I didn't like the sound of it. Jesus had said the oddest things during dinner that night. Things like the bread was His body, as He tore the small flat loaves apart. How horrible! Now He was using the word *glorify*. It sounded heavy.

I thought to myself, *Where is Judas? Where? . . . Glorify . . . glorify . . . . An old man in the Capernaum synagogue used that word in strange ways. He had a daughter too. Before I got married I once thought . . . . That synagogue was special before they plastered the west wall. I had helped build that wall back in the year that my wife's father got sick. It was the year, what year? An odd year . . . an old . . . old year*

. . . . My mind was drifting. I could see the gulls over Galilee but what did that have to do with *glorify*? I was so sleepy I was drifting . . . drifting . . . drifting.

The next thing I knew I was being rudely shaken.

"Wake up." Jesus was shaking me. "You've been asleep for a whole hour. Wake up! Couldn't you watch one hour with me?"

"Excuse me Jesus, I'll do better." Jesus left. I could hear Him praying.

James, John, and I listened to Jesus praying. I could hear Him plainly; I listened intently. I vowed I would not go back to sleep. I even prayed along with Him for a long time. He prayed: *I have revealed you to those whom you gave me out of the world. They were yours; you gave them to me and they have obeyed your word. Now they know that everything you have given me comes from you. For I gave them the words you gave me and they accepted them. They knew with certainty that I came from you, and they believed that you sent me. I pray for them. I am not praying for the world, but for those you have given me, for they are yours. All I have is yours, and all you have is mine. And glory has come to me through them. will remain in the world no longer, but they are still in the world, and I am coming to you. Holy Father, protect them by the power of your name—the name you gave me—so that they may be one as we are one. While I was with them, I protected them and kept them safe by the name you gave me. None has been lost except the one doomed to destruction so that Scripture would be fulfilled. I am coming to you now, but I say these things while I am still in the world, so that they may have the full measure of my joy within them. I have given them your word and the world has hated them, for they are not of the world any more than I am of the world. My prayer is not that you take them out of the world but that you protect them from the evil one. They are not of the world, even as I am not of it. Sanctify them by truth; your word is truth. As you sent me into the world, I have sent them into the world. For them I sanctify myself, that they too may be truly sanctified* (John 17:6-19, NIV).

What did He mean when He said He would no longer be in the world? Where would He be? I started praying that God would keep Him in the world. I told God how much I needed Jesus. I couldn't bear the thought of losing Him. I started thinking about all the wonderful times we had experienced together.

I remembered one day when we were all sailing on Galilee and a huge wind came up, pushing a squall or two with a thousand-foot thunderhead on the top. Well, the waves were suddenly about to capsize us and we all yelled, "Hey Master, don't you care if we drown?"

He seemed disappointed in us for a moment, then He stood up and told the sea to calm down, and the wind to be still. Then everything got peaceful after that. Peaceful like it is now. Quiet like it is now.

My mind began to drift again. *That small house we grew up in . . . I loved going up on the roof and staring at the sea until I lost the place where the sea stopped and the sky started. Together they were so blue . . . blue . . . I felt I was floating in the shadows . . . blue . . . blue . . . floating. . . . I floated until . . . .*

Once again I felt someone shaking me.

"Hey, wake up!"

I was jarred back into reality. It was Jesus again.

"Couldn't you watch one hour with me?"

"I'm sorry Jesus," I said.

Jesus went back to pray. I took my coverlet and splashed a little cold water on my face. This time I firmly decided I would not go to sleep. I could stay awake. I heard Him praying.

My prayer is not for them alone. I pray also for those who will believe in me through their message, that all of them may be one, Father, just as you are in me and I am in you. May they also be in us so that the world may believe that you have sent me. I have given them the glory that you gave me, that they may be one as we are one: I in them and you in me. May they be brought to complete unity to let the world know that you sent me and have loved them even as you have loved me.

Father, I want those you have given me to be with me where I am, and to see my glory, the glory you have given me because you loved me before the creation of the world.

Righteous Father, though the world does not know you, I know you, and they know that you have sent me. I have made you known to them, and will continue to make you known in order that the love you have for me may be in them and that I myself may be in them (John 17:20-26, NIV).

He was praying for all believers. Then I remembered something Jesus had said earlier in the evening. He had quoted Zechariah 13:7: *Strike the shepherd and the sheep will be scattered.*

What did that mean? Suddenly I felt like the night was unbelievably heavy. Was something about to happen? The thought raced into my mind, *Where was Judas?*

Judas. That no-good Judas! I tell you I hadn't trusted him since he created a scene when Mary broke her alabaster jar of nard and poured it on Jesus' feet. Judas became incensed. He was the treasurer, you know. He thought only in terms of gold coins, a tightfisted treasurer if there ever was one. He acted like the bag belonged to him. Where was he now?

I often wondered why Jesus hadn't rebuked Judas more severely the night that Judas made Mary feel so bad. Mary had shown so much more maturity. Sometimes I felt as though I hadn't matured at all. Maturity was hard for me. I remembered back at Capernaum the rabbi was always chiding me to be more mature. "Grow up, Simon," he would say. (Like I could just do it on command.) But on the way home from the school that very day I'd stopped by the sea and studied Galilee until I felt like I was going to be swallowed up in the blue. My mind wandered. *There was no blue like Galilee . . . blue . . . blue . . . blue. . . .*

"Wake up," said Jesus. "The Son of Man is betrayed."

I shook off the sleep—why couldn't I stay awake? Through sleep-filled eyes, I suddenly saw Judas—with a bunch of soldiers. Judas kissed Jesus and the soldiers put the wristlocks on Jesus and led Him away. The rest of us scattered into the night shadows. I followed the soldiers, studying them and their prisoner from afar.

Watching Jesus at a distance, I suddenly felt a hot rush of shame sweep my frame. Blood seemed to wash the underside of my face, and I suddenly realized why He had said His heart was heavy and sorrowful. I now realized why He needed so much to pray, and why He had wanted James and John and me to keep faith with Him as He did. This was the ordeal for which He had armed His soul with the sheer love of God. Why could we not watch one hour? Why indeed!

Then I remembered the words of His prayer. He had prayed for five specific things. First He had prayed that God would protect us followers. Later after intrigue, betrayal, and persecution, I knew why He prayed this.

Next, He had prayed that God would give His followers a full measure of joy. This, in many ways, seemed the most unusual of all His prayers. How could Jesus—facing the cross, with all its attendant horrors—even bring up the matter of joy? Now I understand. Joy is not a matter of giddy laughter or superficial emotion. Joy is the understanding that you've acted out your life in a manner set for pleasing someone else. In this case joy came not from feeling happy. No one can do that all the time. But we can act to please God, and in His pleasure is our joy. Jesus was pleasing God even in the torture of His crucifixion. His obedience produced His joy. He wanted that for us as well.

Then Jesus had prayed that the Father would keep His disciples from the evil one. He also prayed that God would *sanctify* us for use. That word got my attention. He actually prayed that God would make us disciples—all of whom were capable of acting in unholy ways—*holy*. He would take ordinary sinners to do the most glorious work. We ordinary folks would use our dingy lives to build His imperishable kingdom.

But the last part of His prayer intrigued me most. He prayed that all of us might be one. I could see the Lord being hustled along among soldiers on His way to die. I was sure He was praying that we might be one.

In time I would come to know this as the true glory of His church. How often would the church be splintered into little fragments of competitive souls? We twelve had often been guilty of this. We were always competing for attention or worse than that, for power.

Once, James and John came right out and asked him if they could have thrones on either side of His when He became King. Talk about competition! The only thing I felt bad about was, did they know I was wondering what my own place would be in that world order?

Now I saw Him once again—this time through the eyes of a betrayer. Soon He would die. His very life would fall drop by drop and every drop would say, "One . . . one . . . one. . . . I pray they may be one."

Yet, oneness is ever a struggle. Oneness demands that we push our personal agendas below His eternal purpose. We are most unlike God when we only try to gain personal power to be used for some selfish benefit.

I could see Him again. His robe was off. The Son of God was naked. The cat-o'-nine-tails was flaying His back. I wept for I could hear in this parable of torn flesh His cry, "Be one!" I knew why He was being beaten; I knew why He was dying. I knew that I must give up all rights to my own personhood and agenda. Only then I could be of use to Him. Then I could truly honor His dying by living out one purpose, by becoming one with all who are willing to honor His prayer: *Be one.*

Pray With Me!

Jesus prayed for us. And in doing so, He set the example for the most important function of a Christian. Without prayer, we are powerless. With prayer, we are connected to the Creator of all things. Though the Bible provides guidelines for our prayers, prayer remains a supernatural and somewhat mysterious experience for us. It is quite simple, yet, at the same time, immensely complex. How does prayer work? When is it effective? Why does it often seem ineffective?

A recent survey conducted by The Gallup Organization and Barna Research Group shows that most Americans pray privately. 21 percent pray three times a day or more; 15 percent pray about twice a day; 36 percent pray about once a day. 9 percent pray several times each week.

Though many people claim to practice it, prayer is still a vastly under-utilized resource in the Christian life. Prayer can be a cry in the midst of a dark night of despair and hopelessness; it can be a triumphant shout of great joy and elation. Unfortunately, it is, at times, an almost emotionless exercise of rote and repetition. Prayer is available to the Christian at all times, so it is logical that its practice would encompass the great variety of emotions and experiences that make up one's life.

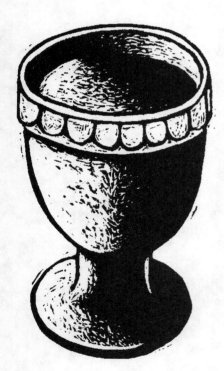

On different occasions, Christ provided examples of praying. One instance of particularly great emotion is the prayer in the Garden of Gethsemane before His crucifixion, detailed in John 17. A.T. Robertson, the well-respected author of many volumes of study of the Greek New Testament, refers to this prayer as "the real Lord's Prayer."[1] On this occasion, Jesus took along His inner circle of disciples—Peter, James, and John—to share His agony of heart and to provide support as He sought help from His Father. Jesus is described with terms such as *very troubled, sorrowful, excessively concerned*, and *agitated*. This prayer of our Savior's great agony touches the soul of all those who are suffering or have suffered. Christians who are alone identify as they read of the Savior whose closest followers could not even stay awake to support Him. Jesus, praying on His face, asked for the power to face "the cup"—a phrase He used to describe His impending death. During this time of prayer He surrendered His will to the will of the Father.

What did Jesus include in this great prayer? The verses of John 17 provide insight into His requests.

First of all, He prayed for Himself—that the Father would glorify the Son so the Son could, in turn, glorify the Father.

He then prayed for His disciples—that they would be protected from the evil one. He prayed they would be sanctified (or set apart) by the Word of God, as they were sent into the world to accomplish the task of telling others about Him.

Lastly, Jesus prayed for future believers—He prayed for you and me.

He prayed that we would be unified so the world would know He was sent to show God's love. He prayed that we would be with Him to behold His eternal glory and share the experience of heaven.

Perhaps the most widely-recognized prayer of Christ is found in Matthew 6 and Luke 11. It is known as The Lord's Prayer, but many scholars prefer to call it The Model Prayer, for Jesus gave the disciples a model by which to pray. Jesus had previously set the example of the importance of prayer, causing one of His disciples to ask for instruction in prayer. The disciples had begun to realize the old public prayers were inadequate for their new life in Christ. The Model Prayer was given in response to the disciples' request, "Lord, teach us to pray," recorded in Luke 11:1. In the verses in Matthew 6 that precede the actual prayer, Jesus provides guidelines for prayer. He warns against meaningless repetition, which was common in pagan religions whose followers thought they would be heard for their abundance of words. Jesus is not condemning all repetition, for he prayed three times in Gethsemane for the same thing. He simply warned against the pagan idea that by many words and repetitions the gods could be wearied into granting requests. Jesus also advised one wishing to pray to go into a room, shut the door, and pray to the Father in secret. Prayer is not to be used to impress God or others. Long, empty phrases are unnecessary, for God already knows what we need—before we ask Him!

In Matthew 6, there are three "Thou petitions" dealing with God, followed by three "Us petitions" dealing with our needs. We are to give God His proper place before turning to our own desires. This prayer gives priority to the requests that God's name be kept holy; His kingdom come, both at the end of time and in submission by those on earth; and His will be done on the earth, just as it is done in heaven. The Luke 11 version omits the words *thy will be done*, but praying for the coming of His kingdom implies the same idea. The three requests for personal needs are: for daily bread; for forgiveness of debts; and for deliverance from evil and temptation. Jesus wanted the disciples to remember God is the source of everything. The forgiveness of obligations is a cornerstone of our relationship with God, for to be unforgiving shows a lack of understanding of our own need for forgiveness. The request concerning temptation is a reminder that it is our tendency to sin, and we need God's help to withstand temptation.

Luke 11: 8-13 provides an important principle for the practice of prayer. Jesus used the story of a friend who goes to another friend's home at midnight asking for bread. The friend refuses the first friend's request because of sleeping children and an already-locked door. Jesus stated that the friend will eventually get up and fulfill the request, not because of the friendship, but because of the seeker's shameless persistence. The problem with our praying is not that we have to overcome a God who is reluctant to hear and answer our prayer. Our persistence, however, indicates our faith, the sincerity of our request, and our belief in a loving, personal God. Jesus concludes the story with the admonition to keep on asking, keep on seeking, and keep on knocking in our prayer relationship with God. We must operate on the basis of our assurance that God will respond to us, perhaps not in the time and manner we desire, but in a manner consistent with His wisdom and love. Most earthly parents want to give their children the very best gifts. How much more our Father in heaven wants to give us what we need! We do not have to coerce gifts from Him.

Write a few sentences describing your attitude toward God when He appears to delay His response to your requests.

One common guide for prayer is easily remembered by the acronym ACTS. We should begin our prayers with Adoration—praising God for Who he is. Confession is the next step, which simply means agreeing with God about the sin in your life. The next area is Thanksgiving, or expressing gratitude to God for all He has done. Supplication is the final step, and is the part of the prayer in which we ask God for help for ourselves and others. A fifth letter, S, may be added to the acronym, for Submission is the final phase of any prayer to God. Can we honestly express willingness to yield to God's plans for us?

A List five things for which you can give God praise and adoration.
1.
2.
3.
4.
5.

C List five things in your life that you feel God would call sinful.
1.
2.
3.
4.
5.

T List five things for which you are thankful today.
1.
2.
3.
4.
5.

S List five requests you have of God.
1.
2.
3.
4.
5.

S List five areas in which you are struggling about submitting to God's will.
1.
2.
3.
4.
5.

Is this prayer outline similar to the way you pray each day? How does it differ from the way you pray? How could using this outline make your prayers more meaningful?

We know much about prayer, but do not fully use this incredible line of power and communication. Prayerlessness is a serious problem in the lives of most Christians today. Rather than being merely an omission in our daily schedules, our neglect of prayer makes a powerful statement about what we believe.

Read the statements below and circle the letters that express your reasons for not praying more often and more diligently.

a. I'm too busy to pray. *I don't have time for you, Lord.*

b. Prayer won't change the outcome of situations. *Praying to you doesn't make any difference, Lord.*

c. I don't know what to say when I pray. *You are unable to understand me if I don't have the right words, Lord.*

d. I am not in a close enough relationship with God to pray. *You only listen to really spiritual people, Lord.*

e. I often forget to pray. *You're not important enough for me to remember, Lord.*

f. I can't seem to remember for whom I need to pray and for whom I have prayed. *I'm too lazy to make and maintain a prayer list, Lord.*

g. I'm too distracted to pray. *I won't slow down enough to concentrate on you, Lord.*

List your three most frequently used excuses for prayer not being a more consistent part of your day.

Joining someone else as a prayer partner can help you strengthen your prayer experiences. Prayer partners togethr learn how to pray as they encourage one another in prayer. Partnership brings greater accountability. Sometimes prayer partners find special times to meet for prayer. Some establish an early morning prayer time at the church, a nearby restaurant or fast food place, or at work or at home. For other prayer partners, prayer is done together by telephone. Others may pray with partners by letters, notes, or even Email on the computer. New prayer networks are growing daily through on-line networks. Many churches, associations, state conventions, and SBC agencies assist with prayer networks.

Bible study classes generally provide time for prayer; some enlist prayer leaders. Some have care leaders who help involve smaller groups in prayer and ministry. The heart of the matter is to share prayer concerns with your Bible study group. Help your group focus on people with needs—physical, spiritual, and emotional. Be sure that prayer is focused on helping class members understand and fulfill their mission for God as a group. Prayer helps classes focus on God's special mission for them as part of their church's overall mission.

PRAYER PARTNERS' COVENANT

We covenant together to become partners in prayer.
Our time for prayer together is

_____.
(date, time)

We covenant to pray for one another and together to pray for the needs of people whose lives we touch each day through our various networks.

Therefore . . . pray for each other . . . . (Jas. 5:16, NIV)

Signed

_____

There are many different words used in the New Testament for prayer. In 1 Timothy 2:1 Paul exhorted Timothy concerning prayer, listing four different terms for prayer. Each of these four tells us something about the process of prayer

The first word for prayer is *request*, or supplication, meaning sincere and humble asking. This word is not used strictly in a religious sense and may refer to requests made to man or God. The second term, *prayers*, specifically refers to requests made to God, not to a fellow man. The third term, *intercession*, means almost the same as supplication, but specifically refers to "intervening or mediating between differing parties, particularly the act of praying to God on behalf of another person." *Thanksgiving* is the last word Paul used, reminding us to thank God for all He has done for us. Too often we utilize prayer as a vehicle only for asking or complaining!

Which term is the most commonly used aspect of your prayers? Which aspect needs more concentration and improvement in your prayer life?

About what are we to pray? Jesus demonstrated that we are to pray about anything—from the smallest daily matters to the weightiest eternal issues. Jesus' Model Prayer exemplifies this important principle. We are also to intercede, or pray, for the needs of others. Intercession is an expression of the concern we have for other people. It is a way to make a difference in what happens in the world. All believers are to intercede for others; it is a sin not to do so! As previously stated, Jesus set the example for intercession by praying for us. We can pray for others regardless of the relationship we have with them.

There are many ways to make intercessory prayer a constant and vital part of daily life. One can commit to pray for those with whom relationships are difficult. One of God's greatest "specialties" is changing the attitude of a heart—ours or the ones for whom we pray! A cancer patient shared that she could not reciprocate the kindnesses of those who drove her to chemotherapy treatments, performed yard work, or provided other services. She could, however, pray for them and any of their special needs of which she became aware through the time she spent with them. One pastor challenged his congregation to pray at least once during the remaining hours of the day for those who responded during the invitation that morning. Many in the congregation that day remembered and responded to his request.

One group of Christian teens at a large high school devised a sign that could be given from one student to another as they walked through the hallways each day. The sign was a closed fist placed over the heart. When given from one Christian student to another, it indicated a need for prayer.

No words had to be spoken; no one had to be stopped in the busy halls between classes. The use of this special sign enabled students to intercede for each other at any time the need was present. The age of instant communication has enabled some youth ministers to carry a beeper for the purpose of intercession for teenagers. The members of the youth group are given cards providing codes for various situations that might occur, warranting prayer. The teen makes a phone call to his or her youth minister who receives the code and prays about the need.

You can practice intercession as you go about the activities of your day. Don't merely think about individuals. Instead, send the thoughts heavenward and pray for God to accomplish His purpose in their lives. While watching television newscasts or reading the daily newspaper, offer prayer for those with special needs. Pray for unborn children of expecting parents, that they will come to know Christ at the earliest possible time. Pray, too, for the parenting skills of the future parents. A Sunday School teacher may choose to distribute a small sheet of paper to class members, asking them to confidentially share their needs and requests. Not only does this action show concern and love, it also provides a good conversation starter for a phone call ("How was that algebra test on Tuesday?") and an opportunity to get to know youth better. Special blessings are abundant for those who are willing to intercede for people they know, as well as for those whom they do not know.

Throughout the New Testament we are given principles to guide our practice of prayer. Listed below are eight basic guidelines to consider as we pray.

1. We must ask according to God's will (1 John 5:14-15).

2. We must ask in faith (Jas. 1:6-7).

3. We must not ask from selfish motives (Jas. 4:3).

4. We must maintain our relationship with Christ (John 15:7).

5. We must pray in Jesus' name (John 14:13-14).

6. We must seek to heal fractured relationships (Matt. 5:23-24).

7. We must be obedient (1 John 3:22).

8. We must confess our sins (Jas. 5:16, Ps. 66:18).

Review the list of prayer guidelines and read the suggested verses. List in the space below the guidelines that are the most difficult for you to follow. Why are these difficult for you? What could you do to overcome these barriers in your prayer relationship with Christ?

What role does faith play in whether or not our prayers are answered? We must have faith for our petitions to be answered. But, we must understand that faith does not always cause our requests to be granted. Christ—in the Garden of Gethsemane—did not have His request granted that the cup of death pass from Him. The apostle Paul asked to be delivered from his "thorn in the flesh" but, instead, was instructed to rest in God's sufficient grace. Even so, believers must not pray without faith. We must pray with the faith that God is looking out for our best interests. Our faith relationship with God through Jesus Christ is one of trust and dependence. We may not see or understand His activities (or lack of them) in our lives. But, we must believe He is taking care of us with love and compassion. Our trust in Him must be child-like, knowing He is our Father in heaven who loves us and cares for us.

There are occasions in Scripture when prayer is described as fervent or earnest prayer. In Acts 12 we are told of Peter's imprisonment by Herod Agrippa I, the grandson of Herod the Great. Herod had already executed James and intended to do the same to Peter. Scripture tells us the church prayed fervently on Peter's behalf as they met at the house of Mary, the mother of John. The situation was desperate, so the prayer was earnest. The Greek word used here to describe this type of praying denotes straining or stretching. (We can more clearly understand the idea as we recall the ancient rack of stretching and torture.) In a miraculous event, Peter was rescued by an angel of the Lord as he slept in his cell, and even those who were praying for his deliverance found it hard to believe he had truly been rescued!

The same form of the word *earnestly* is also used in Luke 22:44, as Luke gives his account of Jesus' prayer in the Garden of Gethsemane before his arrest and crucifixion—*And being in anguish, he prayed more earnestly, and his sweat was like drops of blood falling to the ground*. It is unknown whether there was blood in this sweat, or if the sweat was in the form of great drops, but Luke clearly describes the anguish of Christ's knowledge of His approaching death. He prayed in *agony*, the Greek word taken from the word describing the effort involved in the sport of wrestling. This time of prayer was an occasion during which Christ wrestled with all that had occurred and was about to occur in His life. Can we not identify on a human plane with such intense emotion and wrestling with God in our prayers?

What is the difference between *prayer* and *fervent prayer*? First, the effort put forth in fervent prayer is much greater. Secondly, the attitude brought to the prayer is generally more open and earnest. The third difference is the tremendous intensity of fervent prayer. Lastly, fervent prayer is much more focused and concentrated.

What is your "prayer history"? Can you look back over your life and identify critical times in your life and remember the role of prayer in those times? Consider the following categories and write any recollections of the role of prayer in these situations in your life.

1. Salvation: Do you remember praying to receive Christ? What do you remember about your prayer life as a new Christian?

2. Rededication: Has there been a time of significant recommitment or rededication in your life? What do you remember about your communication with God during this time?

3. Vocation: Did you pray about God's will for your life in terms of your occupation? How did He make His plan known to you? If you are not yet working full-time, how do you pray about God's plan for your life's work?

4. Life mate: If you are married, what role did prayer play in determining God's choice for your life partner? If you are single, what communication do you have with God concerning your singleness?

5. Relationships: Have you prayed about important and/or difficult relationships in your life? How did God work in your life concerning these relationships?

6. Health: Has there been a time when you prayed for God's intervention in your health or the health of a loved one? How did God respond to your prayers? How did you respond to God's response?

7. Submission: Has there been a time in your life when you came face-to-face with the reality that you cannot direct your life on your own terms? How did you realize that God must be the one in control of your life? How did you communicate your thoughts to God?

From a practical standpoint, why do we pray? Because we need peace in a hectic, and often bewildering, world! Pressures come from every aspect of our lives. Some of the greatest stresses originate with those we love the most. The only way to have peace in these experiences is through Christ.

Life cannot be reduced to a formula. Yet, Paul presented a clear statement of what happens when we pray. We are not to worry or be anxious. We are to make adequate preparations, but not worry. To understand the difference between preparation and worry, consider this example: Anna has baked a cake for the Youth Choir bake sale. She follows the recipe carefully, using all recommended ingredients in the correct amounts. The oven is heated to the correct temperature. As she places the cake in the oven, Anna knows she has made all the necessary preparations. However, if she constantly frets about the cake, running back and forth from her room to the kitchen to open the oven door, she has crossed the line from preparation to worry and anxiety. Instead of worrying, we are to let our requests be made known to God and to prepare as He leads. By doing so, He will give us His peace. We cannot produce this peace, and our minds cannot understand it. God's peace is beyond our power to attain, understand, or imagine, but it is not beyond His power to give it to us. It encompasses acceptance and assurance within one's heart and mind, regardless of the circumstances. This peace guards (like a military guard) and protects us against everything. This peace is available to us through prayer.

List below some persons and/or things in your life about which you are anxious or worried. Determine to spend time today making these requests known to God. Thank Him for the peace He promises to give to you.

Most Christians fail to see the miraculous nature of their prayers—often forgetting that the very process of prayer is inherently supernatural. Our requests do not even have to be expressed in words, for God tells us in Romans 8:26 that the Holy Spirit Himself intercedes for us with groans that words cannot express. What a marvelous provision for one's prayer life!

In their book, *Truth on Trial*, Dr. Sam and Ginny Cannata, now retired career missionaries of the International Mission Board, write of one of the miracles of prayer they experienced while Dr. Cannata was imprisoned in

Ethiopia. There was much tension among the guards as Ginny and the children visited Sam in prison one day. The family desired to play a tape from a prayer service in the United States that would provide encouragement for Sam. They feared, however, that the preacher on the tape would mention the Cannatas' names or his Ethiopian situation, which would cause difficulty with the nearby officers who understood English fairly well. As the preacher began to speak about Ethiopia, the Cannatas listened with care, but there seemed to be a skip, or long blank spot, in the tape. When the voice returned, prayers were being offered for the mission families in Ethiopia, but the Cannatas' names were not mentioned. With relief, they finished listening to the tape, prayed together, and left. That same day, Ginny took the tape to her afternoon mission meeting, telling them what had occurred in the prison that morning. That afternoon, however, there was not a blank space on either side of the tape. The Cannatas and the needs of the Ethiopian mission were among the first items mentioned in the prayer time! Because of that experience they were reminded of God's omnipotence in meeting needs. In the morning, the need was for silence. In the afternoon, the need was for the assurance that friends in the states were praying for them. All prayers on their behalf were heard. All needs were met through these prayers of many believers![2]

> Do we understand the ways God responds to our prayers? A church printed the following paragraph in its newsletter:
> If the request is wrong, God says, "No."
> If the timing is wrong, God says, "Slow."
> If you are wrong, God says, "Grow."
> But if the request is right, the timing is right, and you are right, God says, "Go!"
>
> You may think this is an oversimplification of the issue of God's responses to our prayers. However, it provides food for thought. What do we do when the answers to our prayers don't come as we expect? What do we do when God tells us to wait? Those times may be the most difficult of all to many believers.

Consider the following truths for those times when it seems God is delaying a *yes* or *no* answer and your life seems to be on hold. In times of waiting, we must rely on what we know is true. We must stand firmly on the will of God as expressed in His Word. We can never go wrong by depending upon these truths expressed in the Bible.

1. Reaffirm your initial faith/trust in God (1 Pet. 1:8-9).
2. Rest upon the basic promise of God's presence (1 Cor. 1:9).
3. Recognize that God knows your situation (Matt. 10:29-31).
4. Be still and seek to store strength for whatever lies ahead (Isa. 40:31).
5. Remember that life on earth is temporary (2 Cor. 4:16-18).
6. Rely on the sovereignty of God (Rom. 8:37-39).

As we pray, what are the practical guidelines to remember?
1. Tell God the truth. He already knows what is on your heart, but He

wants to hear it from you.

2. Stay up to date with your communication. Talk to God as if He were physically walking beside you at all times. Don't delay taking your concerns to Him. Do it immediately.

3. Acknowledge the sin in your life of which you are aware and ask God's forgiveness. Ask God to show you the sin you have overlooked.

4. Praise Him for being God and thank Him for His availability to you and His presence with you.

Think of prayer "actions" you can take that grow out of prayer. List them. Pray about those actions as part of your prayer time. Consider how those actions can or should involve others, such as people in your Bible study group. How many of the actions will you take individually? How many of these actions will you take with someone else? Pray to discover ways to link up with someone else in responding to the prayer needs you have identified.

As we grow in faith we learn more about prayer. We begin to understand how God speaks to us. We become more conversant with God in our daily lives. This process of growth should never end. We must never assume to know all there is to know about prayer. May our plea always be "Lord, teach us to pray."

stretching

What changes in your prayer life do you believe God desires you to make as a result of what you have considered in this chapter's study? List them in the space below.

1. A.T. Robertson, Word Pictures in The New Testament, Vol. I,III,V
2. Sam and Ginny Cannata, Truth on Trial (Nashville, TN, 1978), 77-78.

chapter 3

Love One Another

Men act certain ways when they are always together that may be too frank for a polite society. Sometimes courtesy and good hygiene are virtually non-existent.

For example, walking along on a hot day in the desert sun you first notice the odor of sweat and then, after a little while, you don't. It's when you quit noticing the odor that you know the problem is most severe. Still there's not much you can do about it, so you don't bring up stuff like that. Everybody just recognizes that all of us have the problem. It's best not to get self-righteous and start acting like you're not as bad off as someone else. Fact is, you are.

Worst of all are the feet. A thirty-mile day in a pair of sandals, during the dry season—well you really don't want to know how bad the feet can get. A couple of my comrades, whose names shall remain anonymous to protect their nearly saintly reputation, always had a little habit of shuffling on the trail, sometimes scrubbing the ground instead of walking on it. These guys were, at first, just dusty—then later in the day they were black nearly up to their knees. It wasn't so bad on those days when we camped out by a stream or in a small town where there was a watering hole. But in towns where no public watering place was accessible, well, you slept sometimes with dirty feet.

On Thursday morning—the final Thursday before Jesus' crucifixion—He sent John and me into Jerusalem to prepare things for the Passover meal. I call that Thursday "Odd Thursday." All day long the oddest things happened! For instance, Jesus told us that in Jerusalem we would meet a man carrying a large jar of water. We were to follow him to the house where he went and tell the host of that house we were going to celebrate the Passover supper there.

So we went into the city looking for a man carrying a water pot. Most people who carried water were women, so our search was not as hard as you might think. Twice we thought we caught sight of such a man, but in both cases it turned out to be a hefty woman. We knew we needed to start being a little more selective and a little less impulsive.

Finally, we caught sight of a man with a heavy beard and a huge water pot. We followed him to a rather large house. I mean, we're talking a big house! It had two stories with a roof garden. It was built in that early Romanesque fashion with poured arches and limestone colors. Anyway, we watched the man disappear through an ornate doorway.

"Well," I said to John, "you go up and ask for the owner of the house like Jesus said, and tell him we need to see the banquet room where we're coming for dinner."

"Nothing doing," said John. "I'm too young; you go ask him."

John was still in his late teens, and you can take my word for it, a teenage disciple is a real pain. Jesus seemed to love John, though. In fact, He made over John a great deal. I didn't understand that. To me, John was a kid. As far as I was concerned, he was not the man to count on when something important needed to be done.

"OK, OK. I'll do it." I walked up to the door and knocked. A man came to the door.

"Yes?"

"Hello, sir, my name is Simon of Galilee and I. . . ."

"Hello, I'm John Mark of Jerusalem."

He was so open and friendly that I immediately felt more confident.

"Well, John Mark, would you show us the banquet room the Master will shortly be needing to observe the Passover?"

"Right this way, sir," he said.

"Just a minute. That kid over there is with me. Hey, Bar-Zebedee, come on."

John ran over and joined us.

"Your son?" John Mark asked me as he motioned toward John.

It always irritated me when anyone thought John was my son. It happened a lot because I was balding a bit, and was a little gray at the temples. And John was so young!

Assuring him that John was not my son, we both followed John Mark through a spacious atrium and then up a flight of stairs. At the top of the stairs we found a wide banquet room. Jesus had told us the room would be furnished and that we were to make preparations for the Passover there. But what I visualized as *furnished* fell considerably short of the real majesty of this upper room. This room was a testament to Roman splendor. Compared to my little house in Galilee, and even to Matthew's comfortable home, I had not seen a house of such magnificence. The banquet area was a series of ornate arches that swept radically out from the center table of polished cedar. The windows were framed and arched by keystoned granite, polished to a glistening shine. The eastern windows looked out over the Fortress Antonia and Olive-Press Park. We often camped in that park and we would probably spend this night there as well.

John and I stood silent. We were all eyes. The beauty of the upper room held a reverence too inspiring to permit speech.

John Mark himself broke the silence. "This is the room, gentlemen. The tableware is on the shelves. Will there be anything else?"

"Uh . . . no," I said, still awed by the grandeur of what I was seeing.

"I'll have the cook prepare the paschal lamb and get the side dishes ready," John Mark said as he left the room.

"Well Johnnie Bar-Z, it's time we set the table."

"Oh, all right." He was reluctant, I could tell. "But give me a hand. Jesus said that we—both of us—were to prepare the upper room."

I set about getting the metal salvers and pewter dishes placed here and there on the shiny cedar table. John had no idea how to set a table. It was clear to me—and I was surprised that Jesus couldn't see it—just how over-protected John was.

"Well, at least fill up the basin with water, so the house servants can wash our feet when we all arrive later tonight."

"Do I have to?" he looked irritated with me. His irritation irritated me. I still wondered why Jesus seemed to dote on this boy. However, to John's credit, he did fill the big jar, but we decided to wait till evening to fill the wash basin. When everything was done, we went back to the rest of the gang.

The thirteen arrived at the upper room just before sundown. I was amazed at the transformation the room had undergone in the brief period of time since John and I had left it. Fresh flowers were on the window ledges, and the huge hanging oil lamps had been lit. Food—glorious-looking food—was now on the table. The odor of the roasted meat was enough to drive a bunch of hungry, itinerant evangelists mad.

As we gathered about the table, Jesus began to sing a psalm.

> *Praise the Lord,*
>
> *Praise, O servants of the Lord,*
>
> *praise the name of the Lord.*
>
> *Let the name of the Lord be praised,*
>
> *both now and forevermore.*
>
> *From the rising of the sun to the*
>
> *place where it sets,*
>
> *the name of the Lord is to be praised.*
>
> *The Lord is exalted over all the nations,*
>
> *his glory above the heavens.* **Psalm 113:1-4, NIV**

We all joined in. We sang it through once while standing, and then we sang it through again as we moved to the reclining couches.

Reclining around the table, we waited for the servant to enter and take the basin and towel and wash our feet so the meal could begin. But no servant came. I wondered, *Who dropped the ball on this one?* It is only proper and an expected courtesy for someone to do this menial but necessary task. Sometimes it seemed like I had to take care of everything.

I whispered to Andrew, "Go downstairs and get a servant to wash our feet." Andrew slipped away from the table and disappeared through the door that led to the stairway. He wasn't gone long when he returned looking a little pained. The servants had been given the night off to have Passover with their families. It looked like one of us would have to do it.

"Andrew . . . ." All of a sudden Andrew wasn't listening to me.

"John," I whispered, turning to the pampered teenager who was lying very close to Jesus. "One of us is going to have to wash feet." John reared up on an elbow and looked at my feet. He sneered. They were dirty, but no dirtier than his. But I could tell he wasn't about to wash anybody's feet.

They would be a formidable challenge, I can tell you, those 26 filthy feet dangling off the ends of the reclining couches. But somebody had to do it. Usually everybody sort of looked to me for leadership when Jesus was off praying, so it just seemed like I should take charge now and designate a foot washer. Now who would it be? Judas? No use asking him. He didn't seem to want to do anything for anybody but himself. Matthew had a nice house of his own, so I doubted he would do it. James Bar-Zebedee refused to look my way. Probably afraid I would ask him!

I briefly thought of taking up the basin and washing all their feet myself. But I was after all, the chief apostle. At least, that's what many said about me. By the way, have I mentioned I was one of those up on the mountain when Jesus was transfigured and stood with Moses and Elijah? I was the first one to call Him the Messiah when we were on retreat at Caesarea Philippi. I was pretty proud of that too. And also I walked on water—or nearly so. Walking on water was not as easy as Jesus made it look.

While I was basking in my vanity, a most amazing thing happened. Jesus got up and went over to the stand. He took the basin, filled it with water, and then He picked up the towel. Returning to the couches, He started washing feet, just like He was a common household slave. Well, we were stunned! He went from one dirty pair of feet to the next, removing our dirty sandals. Jesus made this unenviable task seem like such an act of love filled with so much reverence. Soon the clear water flowed brown in the basin.

Then he came to John and me, the only two left. When Jesus began washing John's feet, inwardly I wanted to say, "Don't wash his feet, Lord. He's a mere teenager with an ego problem." But I held my tongue.

Having washed John's feet, He came at last to me. Perhaps only then did I realize just how dirty my own feet were. It is odd how vanity had caused me to look past my own dirty feet as though they were somehow cleaner than everyone else's feet. Suddenly, I remembered, *Jesus was God's sinless Son!* Yet, there He knelt, starting to undo my sandal straps. I was struck with shame.

John wasn't the only one who had an over-inflated ego. That night a dozen egos led Jesus to teach a lesson by washing feet. We had all been too proud to play the servant.

I felt so ashamed. I drew my feet up under my robe.

"Not my filthy feet," I said to Jesus.

"Peter," He said. "If I don't wash your feet, you have no part in me."

An odd statement! But then it was still Odd Thursday. I took Him to mean that the ultimate measure of our faithfulness was not what we did for Jesus, but what we allowed Him to do for us. Grace is never ours until we are willing to receive it. There is little good in our protesting our unworthiness before God, which is exactly what I was doing in the act of drawing my feet up. No one got into the kingdom because they felt unworthy or humble. Heaven is only gained by crying, "Lord, please save me."

Dirty feet may be ignoble, but the humility of God's Son more than compressed our proud refusals. Jesus' divine nobility was inherent. There was nothing noble in admitting my feet were dirty and He was God's Son. Nobility came only by saying, "Wash me? No part of you unless you wash me? Then wash not just my feet but all of me, Lord."

He unloosed my sandal straps. I first felt His fingers and then the cloth upon my feet. The King held the water and served the slave as though the slave were king and the King were slave.

The water flowed cold across my feet. Joy welled up within my heart. I had a Lord who was quite willing to show me what kingship really meant.

"If I have washed your feet," He said, "Surely you will wash each others' feet."

I wanted to serve Him above all else. I would do it too. I wanted to be like Jesus. No crown, no throne. Just a plain white basin and a willingness to say, "Nothing is beneath my dignity. No act of service can ever be unreasonable if Jesus requires it."

Suddenly I wanted to have my own basin. I wanted to wash the feet of all whom I had lately criticized. I looked at the teenager; I knew where I must start.

Love One Another

The story is told of a young mother who was explaining the upcoming Sunday School promotion day to her six-year-old daughter. "You'll be moving from the room where you now attend Sunday School to the room where the six-year-old children go to Sunday School," explained the mother. "But, mother," protested the child, "how can we leave the five-year-old class when we haven't even been doing 'Be ye kind' very good yet?"

Most of us, regardless of the age of those in our Sunday School classes, are not doing "Be ye kind" very "good" yet—particularly as it pertains to our fellow believers. Though we begin teaching this scriptural truth at the earliest possible age, we don't ever seem to master it. Jesus set the example for the proper relationship with other Christians. It was not an example of one-upmanship, but an example of servanthood. The account of the occasion on which He washed the disciples' feet as recorded in John 13 is a bit shocking when the cultural background is considered. None of the disciples wanted to assume the role of a servant and wash the dirty, smelly feet of his peers. It was considered a lowly and demeaning job. Not one person with social standing beyond that of a servant would even consider such action. Not one person—except Jesus. He quietly took the basin of water and began the task; no questions asked. The picture was worth more than a thousand words, but it can be summarized in these few: "If I have no interest in being a servant, I have no interest in being like Jesus Christ."

One of the most beautiful portraits of Christ in the Scriptures is found in Philippians 2:1-11. In the beginning verses of the chapter, Paul exhorted believers to be unified, like-minded, and to share the same love. They were to share the same purpose in life, being *in full accord*, or "knit together in soul." He continued by encouraging unselfishness characterized by humility that looks out for others' interests as well as his own. In Philippians 2:5 Paul presented the supreme example, Jesus Christ.

Your attitude would be the same as that of Christ Jesus: Who, being in very nature God, did not consider equality with God something to be grasped, but made himself nothing, taking the very nature of a servant, being made in human likeness. And being found in appearance as a man, he humbled himself and became obedient to death—even death on a cross! Philippians 2:6-8

Jesus had the necessary humility and willingness to become a man while He was God. Paul told us He did not think equality with God something to be selfishly grasped. Instead, He chose to relinquish the privileges and rights belonging to Him. Christ's servanthood was not merely an act. It was His true nature and existence. This attitude was manifested in His willingness to suffer death on a cross for us. This is the selfless, servant heart we as

Christians are to exhibit, not merely in our actions, but in our entire being.

Jesus spoke about servanthood on the occasion described in Mark 10:35-45. James and John had asked to sit at Jesus' right and left hands when He came into His kingdom. The other disciples were furious at such a request. Jesus called them together to make His wishes known, saying, *Instead, whoever wants to become great among you must be your servant, and whoever wants to be first must be slave of all. For even the Son of Man did not come to be served, but to serve, and to give his life as a ransom for many.* Once again, Jesus spoke clearly concerning the type of life He wanted His disciples and all believers to live.

Paul continually reinforced Christ's teachings and actions, reminding us as believers that we are to preach Christ as the crucified Lord and ourselves as servants for Jesus' sake. Christ took His place among men as a servant, and we should be prepared to do the same. In 1 Corinthians 9:1 Paul provided an interesting explanation of the possible tension between his freedom in Christ and voluntary slavery for the sake of others. He described his personal freedom as that which gave him the free choice to restrain himself out of his concern for others. He explained his voluntary servanthood to others in that he didn't let all men control his life, for only God controls his life through Christ. However, he became a servant to all in order to win as many as possible to salvation in Christ. Paul explained his desire to understand how others think—to walk alongside them—so he could better grasp their vantage points and communicate with them the gift of life in Jesus. He did it all for the sake of the gospel of Christ. Paul had discovered a basic truth in life: Everyone is a slave to something or someone. A person who chooses to be a servant of Christ has the only true freedom!

It is the desire of Christ that His children have fellowship with each other. The Greek word most commonly used in Paul's letters to describe this fellowship based on faith in Christ is *koinonia*. The commonly accepted meaning of the word *fellowship* in our day has degenerated to refer to any social gathering among our church family involving food and games! In 1 John 1, John wrote of his firsthand knowledge and experience of the life of Jesus Christ. John was an eyewitness to the ministry of Christ. He saw Jesus, touched Him, and knew Him in a personal, intimate way. This knowledge, shared among those who believe in Christ, is the basis of true fellowship.

One of the many aspects of summer youth camp is the fellowship enjoyed among the campers. When teenagers are asked about their camp experiences, common responses include: "I got so close to everybody at camp;" "We were like one big family;" and "I came to love everyone in my youth group." Often, after a few weeks or a few months, the old cliques and divisions in the youth group are again well-established. Why? At camp everyone is focused on Christ and the common bond Christians share through Him. But upon returning home, the focus often shifts to school interests, economic differences, and race. Such was the case with Dan, an eighth grader who had never felt very much a part of his youth group. He attended a different school than the other eighth grade boys in his group at church. He lived miles away from them and had another group of friends during the week. Dan decided at the last minute to go to youth camp. He had not been sure if he wanted to go, for

THE J FILES
YOUTH LEADER EDITION:

FOLLOW CHRIST'S EXAMPLE

by Jane Wilson Brinkley

chapter 1

Follow Me

Objective: Believers in Christ must carefully examine the meaning of Jesus' invitation, *Follow Me* in order to more completely fulfill their mission in God's kingdom.

Preparation

For Step 1: Arrange chairs in circles for team work, and prepare a copy of the following assignment to go in each circle: *Think of a person you know who exemplifies the life of someone who follows Jesus. Which of their actions or attitudes are most Christlike? Share your answers with the group.*
For Step 1 Option: Obtain children's music and a cassette or CD player.
For Step 2: Provide copies of *The J Files*, large sheets of paper, felt-tip markers.
For Step 3: Provide large sheets of paper, felt-tip markers.
For Step 3 Option: Provide a Bible for each team; prepare role-play assignments:
  • *Team 1: An adult is sharing with a friend his hesitations concerning yielding his life to Christ and following Him.*
  • *Team 2: A teenager is sharing with an adult Christian his hesitations concerning yielding his life to Christ and following Him.*
  • *Team 3: A mom and dad are sharing with a youth minister their hesitations about their teen's yielding her life to Christ and following Him.*
For Step 4: Collect lifestyle examples ahead of time.
For Step 5: Duplicate copies of item 1 (handout), "Helps and Hindrances," provide pencils, cassette or CD of "For the Sake of the Call" (or another suitable song), and cassette or CD player.

Procedure

Step 1 (10 min.) Form one or more circles of chairs. Place an assignment card in each circle. As conferees arrive, ask them to select a chair and begin the assignment. After allowing a few minutes for teams to work, state: One of the best ways to understand the meaning of following Christ is to see an excellent example. This study will enable us to see the life of Christ as an example in all areas. Today's session will seek to broaden our thinking about what is involved in Christ's invitation, *Follow Me*.

Step 1 Option: Play children's music as conferees enter. If they look puzzled, assure them they are in the correct conference! When everyone has arrived, state: We are going to begin today's session by playing two children's games based on the concept of following. Lead the group around the room playing "Follow the Leader," making various changes in the way you walk or in your hand motions. Quickly change to a game of "Simon Says," trying to trick them into making mistakes as they follow you. Ask: What are the similarities and differences in the way you followed while playing these games and the way you follow as Christ leads you each day? (*Possible responses include: I played this game with more intensity than I often follow Christ; Christ doesn't try to trick me like this leader did, and so on.*) State: One of the best ways to understand the meaning of following Christ is to see an excellent example. This study will enable us to see the life of Christ as an example in all areas. Today's session will expand our thinking about what is involved in Christ's invitation, *Follow Me*.

Step 2 (15 min.) Divide the group into three teams, providing each with a large sheet of paper and a felt-tip marker. Ask each team to list the things that come to mind when they hear the words *Follow Me*. After a few minutes, call for sharing. Read Luke 9:23-24 aloud from page 15 in *The J Files*. Direct workers to review the three conditions for following Christ and the four sayings of Jesus that are provided in the section that follows. Ask for volunteers to share what is most difficult for them about the standards Christ set forth for discipleship.

Step 3 (15 min.) Have conferees remain in the same three teams, and give a large sheet of paper and a felt-tip marker to each team. Assign one of the following questions to each team: *What hesitations might adults have about abandoning all to Christ and following Him? What hesitations might teenagers have about abandoning all to Christ and following Him? What hesitations might parents have about their teenagers abandoning all to Christ and following Him?* After allowing time for teams to work, ask each team to share its list with the entire group. Ask: How do you think Christ would respond to the problems we have presented?
Ask workers to assist you in providing scriptural responses to several of the responses on the lists. Ask: In what ways can an adult who works with youth set an example of following Christ? Briefly mention the fifteen characteristics of a disciple listed on page 17 of *The J Files*. Encourage workers to take time during the next few days to study these characteristics, the related Scriptures, and complete that self-evaluation activity.

Step 3 Option: Using the same three teams, give each team a Bible and a card on which is written one of the role-play assignments. Instruct each team to provide in some way a scriptural response to the hesitations expressed by the person in the assigned role play. After allowing time to prepare, ask each team to role-play its assignment. Ask: Do you identify with the hesitations expressed in any of these situations? Why or why not?

Step 4 (10 min.) Before the session, secure (from newspapers, magazines, and so on) current examples of teens and adults whose behavior in particular situations has shown an understanding of Jesus' invitation, *Follow Me*. You may want to include the examples provided on page 21 in *The J Files*. After sharing these examples, ask: What do the actions of these individuals show about their understanding of Christian discipleship? Allow workers to share examples, also.

Step 5 (10 min.) Distribute a copy of the handout, "Helps and Hindrances" (item 1) to each person, along with a pencil. Instruct conferees to consider any attitudes and lifestyle practices that help or hinder them in their personal quest to follow Christ. Encourage them to determine what they need to do to increase the positives and eliminate the negatives they have listed. After allowing time for thoughtful consideration, ask for volunteers to share their ideas. Play "For the Sake of the Call" by Steven Curtis Chapman or another song that relates to the challenge of following Christ.
Close with a prayer of commitment.

chapter 2
Pray With Me

Objective: Christians must understand and utilize prayer to obtain the strength to live as Jesus' representatives in today's world.

Preparation

For Step 1: Write the following assignment on the chalkboard or a large piece of paper: *On the sheet of paper, complete the following statements. The best thing about prayer is . . . . The most difficult thing about prayer is . . .;* provide pencils and paper.

For Step 1 Option: Provide pencils and paper. Write the following situations on separate sheets of paper: *High school senior who wants a date to homecoming; middle-aged adult with an ill parent; basketball coach wanting to win a big game; parent of a rebellious teen.* (You may duplicate topics if you expect a large group.)

For Step 2: Provide Bibles, large sheets of paper, and felt-tip markers.

For Step 3: Provide copies of *The J Files*.

For Step 3 Option: Provide paper and crayons.

For Step 4: Duplicate copies of item 2 (handout) "The Bible Speaks About Prayer," provide pencils.

For Step 5: Provide copies of *The J Files*, paper, pencils.

Procedure

Step 1 (10 min.) Before conferees arrive, place a sheet of paper and a pencil in each chair. As they enter, direct the workers' attention to the assignment you have written on the chalkboard or paper. After all conferees have arrived and responded to the statements, direct them to make a paper airplane from their sheet of paper and fly it toward others in the group. Each person will then pick up a paper airplane, read the responses, and share them with the group. State: We have various ideas concerning prayer. Today's session will explore what Jesus taught His disciples about prayer and how to utilize this source of communication with God.

Step 1 Option: In the center of each circle of chairs place one of the papers with a situation written on it, extra paper, and pencils. As conferees arrive, instruct them to select a chair according to the topic in the center of the circle. State: Consider the situation you have chosen. Write a brief dialogue of a conversation that might take place between God and the person described. Choose two team members to read the dialogue to the large group. After allowing a few minutes for teams to work, ask each group to share its work. State: We have various ideas concerning prayer. Today's session will explore what Jesus taught His disciples about prayer and how to utilize this source of communication with God.

Step 2 (10 min.) Divide the group into teams (one person can be a team). Provide a Bible, a large sheet of paper, and a felt-tip marker for each team. Assign one of the following Scripture passages to each team: John

17:1-25, Luke 11:1-13, and Matthew 6:5-15. Instruct each team to read the assigned passage and list several of the principles concerning prayer taught in the passage. After allowing time to complete the assignment, ask each team to share its ideas. Ask: How would your prayer life change if you followed these principles of prayer? Allow time for volunteers to share ideas.

Step 3 (15 min.) Read 1 Timothy 2:1 aloud to the group, writing on the chalkboard the four words for prayer that are found in this verse (*requests, prayers, intercession, thanksgiving*). Ask conferees to help determine working definitions for each word. (See page 33 of *The J Files* for information to assist in this exercise.) Direct workers' attention to the aspects of prayer represented by the acronym ACTS(S) as described on page 31 of chapter 2 of *The J Files*. As you review the acronym together, write the words on the chalkboard. Ask workers to share some of the experiences they have had while involved in any of these aspects of prayer. (Be prepared to share one or two of your personal experiences as the group members think about sharing some of their own.) Ask: Is most of your experience in praying found in only one or two of these aspects of prayer? Why or why not? (*Possible responses include: I spend most of my time asking God for something; I rarely show adoration to God in my prayer time; I often forget to confess my sins; and so on.*) Ask: How do you think God feels when He hears you pray? What does He think about the way you pray and the things you include (and don't include) in your prayers? Allow time for responses.

Step 3 Option: Instead of asking the final two questions in Step 3 concerning God's response to our prayer, distribute a sheet of paper and crayons to each worker. Give the following instructions: Draw a picture of how you think God looks as He listens to your prayers. Is He puzzled? saddened? joyful? Use your imagination! Ask volunteers to share their drawings with the group.

Step 4 (15 min.) Distribute a copy of the handout, "The Bible Speaks about Prayer," (item 2) and a pencil to each conferee. Instruct them to read each statement and determine whether they agree or disagree with it. After allowing time for individual work, ask for volunteers to read each statement and share their opinions. Use the Scripture references to point out what the Bible says about each statement.

Step 5 (10 min.) Distribute a piece of paper and a pencil to each worker. Direct attention to the six actions listed on page 40 (what to do while we wait for God to answer our prayers) and pages 40-41 (practical guidelines to remember) of *The J Files*. Read them aloud or ask conferees to read them silently. Ask: What strengths in your prayer life have you discovered during this study? What weaknesses in your prayer life have you discovered? On the piece of paper, write three things you can do daily to make your prayer communication with God stronger and more effective. After allowing time for conferees to write their responses, close in a time of silent prayer.

chapter 3
Love One Another

Objective: Love and servanthood characterize our relationships with other believers when we follow Christ's example.

Preparation

For Step 1: Make assignment cards on which are written these two assignments: (1) *Make a list of ten undesirable tasks you might be asked to do in your church;* (2) *Make a list of ten undesirable tasks you might be asked to do for a friend.* Provide several large sheets of paper and felt-tip markers; arrange chairs.

For Step 2: List these Scripture passages and questions on the chalkboard: *Philippians 2:1-11; Mark 10:35-45; 1 Corinthians 9:19-23. What do these passages tell about the behavior of those who know Christ? What personal challenges do they provide?* Provide Bibles, paper, and pencils; prepare *koinonia* minilecture; write *fellowship* letters on sheets of paper.

For Step 3: Write the following words on cards: *unforgiveness, jealousy, prejudice, pride.* Write on the chalkboard: *Role-play a situation in which your assigned trait interferes in the fellowship of a church.*

For Step 3 Option: Using the "Whom would you call?" questions (from pages 49-50 of *The J Files*) write the questions on slips of paper and place them in a small basket.

For Step 4: Write the following phrases or Scripture references on slips of paper and place them in a basket: *Prayed with one another; Acts 12:5; broke bread together; Acts 2:42; shared everything; Acts 2:44; ministered to sick and/or grieving; James 5:13-15; spoke on behalf of each other; Philemon 17-19; opened their homes to each other; 1 Corinthians 16:19; organized to meet needs; Acts 6:2-5; cared for widows and orphans; James 1:27.*

For Step 4 Option: Instead of the activity involving actions and Scriptures in step 4, write only the actions on the slips of paper and place them in a basket. Provide felt-tip markers and large sheets of paper.

For Step 5: Duplicate copies of item 3 (handout) "Jesus In My Church;" provide pencils.

Procedure

Step 1 (10 min.) Before conferees arrive, place chairs in circles with an assignment card, large sheet of paper, and a felt-tip marker in each circle. As conferees arrive, instruct them to select a chair and begin work on the assignment provided. After allowing time for work, ask each group to share its responses. Ask: What makes these tasks undesirable? Have you ever performed these tasks? Why or why not? State: Today's session relates to the importance of loving and serving others in the body of Christ.

Step 2 (15 min.) Distribute Bibles, pencils, and paper to each team, assigning them one Scripture passage and instructing them to answer the related questions. Ask each team to report its findings.

Present a brief explanation of *koinonia* and of 1 John:1 from page 48 of *The J Files*. Distribute one letter of the word *fellowship* to every two or three workers until all letters are gone. State: Think of one example of true biblical fellowship that begins with your letter. (*Possible responses: F—finding ways to serve other Christians; P—praying with someone about a need; and so on.*) Direct workers to attach the letters to a focal wall to spell the word *fellowship* as they explain their part of the acrostic. Encourage conferees to read during the coming week the list of the things Christians have in common and the related Scripture passages on page 49 of *The J Files*.

Step 3 (10 min.) Divide into four teams and distribute one word to each team, directing attention to the instructions on the chalkboard. After teams present their role plays, allow conferees to guess the trait depicted by the team. Then ask: What is your experience with these characteristics and their effects on the fellowship of a church? How do you think Christ views such actions and attitudes? What impressions do unbelievers receive from such actions and attitudes?

Step 3 Option: If your group is from one church, you may choose to use this option in addition to the activity in step 3. Allow conferees to draw a question from the basket and answer it aloud. Allow others to share their responses.

Step 4 (15 min.) Ask each conferee to draw a slip of paper and match the action of the early believers with the correct Scripture reference. Provide Bibles for looking up Scripture passages. (In the listing above, the correct reference follows the action.)

Step 4 Option: Divide into two teams. State: We are going to play a game of artist charades in which a person from each team will draw a slip of paper on which is written one way believers in the early church related to each other. That person will illustrate the action on paper and his or her team will try to guess it within one minute. The team with the most correct responses wins. After all slips of paper have been drawn and guessed, ask for additional ideas for ministries in these areas. You may want to share with them the ministry ideas from *The J Files* (pages 56-58).

Step 5 (10 min.) Distribute pencils and a copy of the handout, "Jesus In My Church," to each person. State: In today's session we have considered the ways of servanthood and love. Answer these questions concerning how Jesus might interact in your church, as well as your task as His representative. Allow time for conferees to write their responses.
Close the session with a prayer of commitment.

chapter 4
Love Your Neighbor

Objective: Believers must follow Christ's example to love others and seek to meet their needs.

Preparation

For Step 1: Place several newspapers in every third or fourth chair; write the following instructions on the chalkboard: *In the newspapers you were given, look for: (1) individuals or organizations who are meeting the needs of others; and (2) needs that could be met by teenagers.*

For Step 1 Option: Pre-record video clips of news stories that feature individuals or organizations ministering to others. On the chalkboard or large piece of paper write the following instructions: *As you watch the recorded news stories, look for (1) individuals or organizations who are meeting the needs of others; and (2) needs that could be met by teenagers.* Provide paper and pencils; secure a TV/VCR.

For Step 2: Provide copies of *The J Files*, paper, and pencils; write *Today's Samaritans* on the chalkboard or a large piece of paper.

For Step 2 Option: Provide paper and pencils.

For Step 3: Write on three-by-five-inch cards one of the following statements: *God's grace and love extend to the entire world, not just to those who love Him; Man was created in God's image and is, therefore, valuable; All human beings have sinned;* and *Jesus came to earth to save man.* On each card, write also these questions: *Does any particular group of people come to mind when you read this statement? What are the implications of this statement to a theology of helping others?* Provide paper and pencils.

For Step 4: Write on the chalkboard or a large piece of paper the following questions: *Have you seen any needs of the people in these groups met in an especially unique or successful way? How?* Provide pencils and duplicate copies of item 4 (handout), "My Neighbors."

Procedure

Step 1 (15 min.) Before conferees arrive, place newspapers in chairs. As conferees arrive, ask them to form teams and complete the assignment as written on the chalkboard. After allowing time for team work, ask groups to report their findings. Ask: Did you discover needs that you felt were not your obligation to meet? Did you discover persons you felt did not deserve to be helped? Why did you feel that way? After hearing responses from conferees, state: Jesus gave us a clear command about meeting needs and loving our neighbors. In today's session, we will examine His teachings and the example He set in loving others.

Step 1 Option: Instead of using newspapers as suggested in step 1, play the videotaped news stories previously recorded. Before playing the tape, direct conferees' attention to the instructions you have written on the board. Provide paper and pencils for each person, instructing them to jot down their responses to the statements as they watch the video. After the video is over, call for sharing.

Step 2 (15 min.) Instruct conferees to read the explanations of the story of the Good Samaritan and the account of Jesus' encounter with the Samaritan woman at the well found on pages 64-66 of *The J Files*. Ask for suggestions in completing a list of people in today's world that would be likely substitutions in the two biblical accounts just examined. After completing the list, ask: In what ways do we shun these persons today? Direct conferees to turn to page 66 in *The J Files* and complete the survey "How Big Is Your World?" If books are not available, distribute paper and pencil to each person, directing them to write *F*, *S*, *R*, or *N* (according to the instructions provided in the book) after you read each of the group names out loud. State: Sometimes we purposely make our worlds small enough to omit groups we consider undesirable. What do you think Christ would say to the Christian whose world has become too small?

Ask them to complete the exercise in the box on page 67 to discover some ways Jesus responded to needs and showed love for his neighbors.

Step 2 Option: After reviewing the stories on pages 64-66 of *The J Files* as suggested in step 2, divide the group into at least two teams, assigning one of the stories to each team. Give the following directions: Write a brief story—in a setting in today's world—that teaches the same principle as the biblical account you were assigned. Provide paper and pencil for each team. After allowing time for work, ask each team to read its story and explain why those particular characters were chosen.

Step 3 (15 min.) Distribute to four individuals the cards you have prepared with statements and questions, a sheet of paper, and a pencil. Ask each cardholder to form a team to discuss the statement and answer the questions. After teams have completed the assignment, allow each to share ideas. Then ask: What are some of the barriers we face as we try to live according to these four statements? (Possible responses: *Fear, prejudice, not enough time, not enough interest, and so on.*) What do you think Christ would say about these barriers?

Step 4 (10 min.) Distribute a pencil and a copy of the handout, "My Neighbors," to each person. Direct conferees to choose another person with whom to work. Ask each pair to answer the questions (written on the chalkboard or paper) about each of the groups listed on the handout. After allowing time for conferees to work through the list, ask them to share their ministry ideas with the entire group. Encourage conferees to write down ideas in order to put them into action.

Step 5 (5 min.) Instruct conferees to review once again the handout, "My Neighbors." Direct them to circle any of the ideas that they will commit to put into action during the next two weeks. Also, circle the name of any ministry group whose needs they will commit to trying to meet in the coming weeks. Beside the name of that group, direct them to write the greatest barrier they will have to overcome to meet those needs. Close by reading Matthew 25:37-40 aloud as conferees bow their heads in prayer.

chapter 5
I Am Sending You

Objective: God's plan is for Christians to carry out the Great Commission and to train others to do so.

Preparation

For Step 1: Provide paper and pencils. Write the following assignment on the chalkboard or a large piece of paper: *List occupations that utilize the principle of internship or apprenticeship.*

For Step 1 Option: Provide paper and pencils; write the following assignment on the chalkboard or a large piece of paper: *List projects or goals you did not meet because you delayed in starting them.*

For Step 2: Make three team assignment cards with the following assignments: *Team 1.—John 20:19-21, John 21:15-19; Team 2.—Matthew 28:18-20; Team 3.— 2 Corinthians 5:16-20.* Write the following questions on the chalkboard: *What is the commission described in the passage(s) assigned your team? List some ways your team can fulfill this commission.* Provide copies of *The J Files*, Bibles, pencils, and paper.

For Step 3: Write on a chalkboard or large piece of paper the following six characteristics of Jesus as found in *The J Files: Jesus embodied the truth; Jesus desired to serve; Jesus believed in teaching; Jesus knew the Scriptures; Jesus understood human nature;* and *Jesus mastered the art of teaching.* Write on slips of paper the twelve mentoring principles of Paul from pages 89-90 of *The J Files* and place the twelve slips in a basket. Provide paper, pencils, and copies of *The J Files*.

For Step 3 Option: Provide paper, pencils, and copies of *The J Files*.

For Step 4: Duplicate copies of item 5 , "Me—A Mentor?" (handout) Provide pencils and copies of *The J Files*. Select a well-known hymn of submission to be sung at the close of the session.

Procedure

Step 1 (10 min.) Before youth workers arrive, arrange chairs in groups of two or three, placing a piece of paper and pencil in each group of chairs. As workers arrive, direct their attention to the chalkboard or paper on which you have written the assignment. Allow time for teams to work, then call for sharing. State: Throughout history, persons wanting to enter certain vocations have been required to spend a time of apprenticeship with someone experienced in that vocation. God's plan to evangelize the world involves a similar concept of Christians training others, who will also eventually train others. The focus of today's session is to examine our call to action as Christians, and our need to train those younger in the faith.

Step 1 Option: Instead of the activity suggested in step 1, refer conferees to the assignment you have written on the chalkboard or paper. After allowing time for teams to work, ask each to share its responses. State: As

Christians, most of us know more about how we are supposed to respond to the Great Commission than we are actively doing. In today's session we will examine our call to immediate action to fulfill this command of Christ, as well as our need to train those younger in the faith.

Step 2 (15 min.) If necessary, combine the teams formed in step 1 to make three teams. Present a minilecture concerning the four basic ways by which others will be able to see our commitment to following Christ's example. (See pages 84-85 in *The J Files*.) Provide Bibles, pencils, and paper and give out assignments. After allowing time for work, ask each team to share its responses. (You may choose to supplement their responses with information from the explanation of these Scripture passages found in *The J Files*.)

Step 3 (20 min.) Refer conferees to the six characteristics of Christ that are on a focal wall. Briefly define each characteristic, using information from pages 88-89 of *The J Files*. State: Think of someone who has taught or trained you in the Christian life. Which of these six characteristics of Christ did these persons show? Call for workers to share their responses.
Briefly explain Paul's mentoring relationship with Timothy. Direct workers' attention to the basket containing the strips of paper with Paul's principles of mentoring. Using the teams they have already formed, ask a member of each team to draw a slip of paper from the basket until all are taken. Provide paper and pencils. Direct each team to create a brief role play to illustrate the mentoring principle they have drawn from the basket.
Allow time to work; as role plays are presented, the other teams will guess which principle is being illustrated. After all role plays have been presented, compare the lists with the listing from *The J Files*.

Step 3 Option: After examining the six characteristics of Christ as detailed in step 3, direct workers to the checklist for each of the four chapter topics found on pages 92-93 of *The J Files*. Ask conferees to complete the checklist with honesty. Call for volunteers to share their responses.

Step 4 (15 min.) Present a brief summary of the Christian's responsibility to bear fruit as expressed in John 15:1-17. (See page 92 of *The J Files*.) Call workers' attention to the seven mentoring situations listed on page 90 of *The J Files*. Distribute pencils and copies of the handout, "Me—A Mentor?" Instruct each worker to complete the handout by circling and/or underlining their potential strengths and weaknesses in a mentoring situation. Encourage workers to think prayerfully before answering the *yes* or *no* question concerning their willingness to become a mentor. Allow time for each person to complete the handout.
Close in a prayer of dedication and by singing "Take My Life, Lead Me, Lord," (#287, Baptist Hymnal, 1991), or another hymn of submission.

HELPS and HINDRANCES

These things in my life help me as I follow Christ:

These things in my life hinder me as I follow Christ:

What I think Christ wants me to do to more completely follow Him:

Item 1 (Handout)
The J Files Leader Edition
© Copyright 1997—Convention Press   All rights reserved. Code 5130–48

The Bible Speaks About Prayer

Consider each of the following statements.

Write *agree* or *disagree* in the blank before each statement.

_____ 1. Praying in faith is a vital condition for answered prayer.

_____ 2. God hears requests asked according to His will.

_____ 3. It is the Christian's responsibility to seek to heal broken relationships before praying.

_____ 4. Selfishness interferes with answered prayer.

_____ 5. Praying in Jesus' name is an essential part of prayer for the Christian.

_____ 6. Obedience to Christ does not affect one's prayer life.

_____ 7. Unconfessed sin is a hindrance to our communication with God.

_____ 8. We must maintain our relationship with Christ is order to have a productive prayer life.

Item 2 (Handout)
The J Files Leader Edition
© Copyright 1997—Convention Press   All rights reserved. Code 5130–48

Jesus in My Church

If Jesus was a member of your church, in what activities would He be involved?

What position(s) would He hold? On what committees would He serve?

Where and with whom would He sit during worship services?

What might people say about Him in your church and city?

Since Jesus doesn't attend your church, but you do, list two things He would like to see you do there.

Item 3 (Handout)
The J Files Leader Edition
© Copyright 1997—Convention Press   All rights reserved. Code 5130–48

MY NEIGHBORS

Here are ten groups of people to whom you may minister.
Beside each group, jot down some ministry ideas.

- Physically disabled

- Mentally disabled

- Senior adults

- Economically disadvantaged

- Illiterate

- Internationals

- Chronically ill

- Legal offenders

- Victims of natural disaster

- Families in other difficult situations

Item 4 (Handout)
The J Files Leader Edition
© Copyright 1997—Convention Press   All rights reserved. Code 5130–48

ME—A Mentor?

- Circle the principles that would be your areas of strength if you choose to be a mentor to someone new in the faith.

- Underline your areas of weakness.

    Provide encouragement

    Pray for them

    Accept them as co-workers

    Provide doctrinal instruction

    Prepare them for situations they would face

    Advise them concerning personal behavior

    Allow them to gain experience in working without you

    Trust their judgment

    Show respect for them and affirm them before others

    Lead by example

    Point them to the highest goal of God's calling

    Challenge them to share with and train others

- Are you willing to consider serving as a mentor?

        yes   no

Item 5 (Handout)
The J Files Leader Edition
© Copyright 1997—Convention Press   All rights reserved. Code 5130–48

his family was considering a move to a church nearer home. During camp week Dan was an integral part of his camp "family" and participated well with everyone in attendance. On the last night at camp he told his Sunday School teacher, "I'm at home with this group. I'm here to stay!" Within a few weeks after camp, however, the same divisions occurred within the eighth grade boys—they went to different schools; they lived in different communities. The "majority group" felt (and acted) superior to Dan. Within a few months, Dan and his family left the church.

We may choose to allow many things to separate us from other Christians: race, cultural background, economic status, education, family size, and beliefs about various issues and past experiences. But, Paul emphasized that believers should be bound together by a common mind. We have many important aspects in common with our fellow believers. Consider the eight commonalities listed below:

> 1. **Our heavenly father** (John 10:29-30, John 14:21,23)
> 2. **Our eternal destiny and inheritance** (John 3:16, 1 Peter 1:3-4)
> 3. **Our experience of salvation** (Rom. 10:9-10, Eph. 2:8-9)
> 4. **The indwelling Holy Spirit** (John 14:16-17, John 15:26)
> 5. **The power to live a Christ-like life** (John 15:7-8, Phil. 4:13)
> 6. **The privilege of communication with God** (Heb. 4:15-16, Phil. 4:6-7)
> 7. **The purpose of our time on earth** (Matt. 28:19-20, Eph. 2:10)
> 8. **The written Word of God** (Heb. 4:12, 2 Tim. 3:16)

Think about the fellowship you share with those in the local body of faith you know as your church. Answer the following questions:

1. Whom would you call if you needed someone to pray for you?

2. Whom would you call if you needed a service need met, such as someone to drive you somewhere or someone to bring food to your home if you were ill?

3. Whom would you call if you needed encouragement?

4. Whom would you call for advice?

5. Whom would you call if you needed a home in which to spend the night and eat a meal?

6. Whom would you call in the middle of the night if you had an emergency?

Jesus spoke clearly when He said, *A new command I give you: Love one another. As I have loved you, so you must love one another. By this all men will know that you are my disciples, if you love one another.* He issued this command as He was preparing for His crucifixion. Knowing there would be a great void because of his ascension to the Father, He commanded His disciples to love each other as He had loved them. No longer could the disciples be identified by their devotion to the physical image of Christ. From that time on they would be identified by their adherence to the kind of love Christ practiced. They were to go beyond the Jewish teaching to love one's neighbor as oneself. Instead, they were to love their neighbors more than themselves, for they were to love as Christ loved. We are not to be known by how we dress, by our customs, or by our peculiar habits—we are to be known by our love! Christ gave the world a criterion by which they could judge us as believers: How much do we love each other?

Check any areas of your life that may prevent others from seeing Christ's love in you.

___the way I speak about fellow Christians

___a negative attitude when my opinion at church isn't accepted by others

___my response to people in need

___my attitude when I feel I have been treated unfairly

___associating with only my closest friends when at church

___willingness to help others who may not be close friends

___critical spirit about others

___jealousy when someone in the church receives attention I feel I deserve

___lack of interest when new people visit our church

___being a poor, uninterested listener when someone shares his or her problems with me

___talking too much about myself and my interests and activities

___an unwillingness to include new church members in responsibilities within the church (serving on committees, teaching, and so on)

Some of the behaviors listed above are a result of an inadequate love for oneself. The forces that contribute to a person's self-love are deeply rooted and can often be complex. Loving oneself is a basic prerequisite for loving others. We are more likely to want others to conform to what we think they should be when we are not happy with who we are. We show our lack of self-love when we are overly critical of others, jealous, unforgiving, and extremely sensitive to what others say and do. Many people navigate life in a perpetually wounded state, continually hurting because of the words and actions of others. This type of life does not demonstrate self-love. A healthy self-love is based on what the Bible tells us about our lives: We are created by God in His image. We were created as capable of having fellowship with God, which is His desire. Christ's death on the cross serves as a constant reminder of our worth to our Creator. Still, many of us have difficulty accepting and loving ourselves. There are many excellent resources available to help us understand our need for self-love. Most pastors and ministers of youth are able to provide appropriate resources when such help is requested.

What difficulties most frequently interfere with the fellowship among believers? In the fourth chapter of James, he asked this question: *What causes fights and quarrels among you?* He suggested that dissension among believers is caused by desires that are not fulfilled and the resulting inner frustrations.

There are other specific attitudes and actions that can be very damaging to a body of believers. One of the primary ones is *an unforgiving spirit.* Even the disciples had trouble understanding the need for forgiveness. The Scripture tells us that Peter asked Jesus for a limit on the number of times he must forgive. Jesus made it clear that forgiveness was not merely an act, but a way of thinking. Keeping track of how many times one has forgiven defeats the purpose of a forgiving spirit. The willingness to forgive others shows an understanding of one's own need for forgiveness. As Christians, we often have a difficult time forgiving other Christians because we think they should know better than to do the things requiring forgiveness. We must remember that we all have sinned and continually stand in need of someone's forgiveness.

Chris Carrier is a man who understands the importance of forgiving others. A former youth minister, Chris was kidnapped at age 10 while living in Miami, Florida. His abductor stabbed him with an ice pick, drove him to a desolate spot, shot him in the head from behind, and left him for dead. Chris, unconscious for six days, awoke the day after Christmas and was rescued by a farmer who discovered him. At age 32, Chris chose to forgive and befriend David McAllister, age 77, who a few months earlier had confessed to the abduction. (Mr. McAllister had been a prime suspect, but there was no physical evidence linking him to the crime.) Chris not only visited Mr. McAllister in a nursing facility, but was the only person waiting at the hospital to pay his last respects after he died. No names of family members were provided by Mr. McAllister before his death. Although Chris was blinded in his left eye as a result of the shooting, he made this statement, "It wasn't hard for me to show compassion, given his circumstances. I moved on. This event will not haunt me all my life."

What are some of the ways people in your church offend you? What are the most common ways you offend people in your church? How willing are you to quickly forgive others?

How does the absence of forgiveness separate you from others in the body of Christ?[1]

Love binds us together. When we experience the forgiveness of God through Christ, we join together with others who have experienced that same forgiveness. We become part of a congregation that in a real sense is a larger family. We also become part of a smaller unit of the family, a Youth Sunday School class—a group of people with whom we most closely bond. Together as a bonded group, we study the Bible, pray, and seek to tell the lost of the joy of God's forgiveness.

Studies show that when bonding does not occur for a new Christian or new church member, that person soon ceases to be involved with the group. Sometimes the bonding becomes interrupted. A youth may drop out for any number of reasons, such as personal or family sickness, trauma or personal tragedy, or (often the case with teenagers) the person was hurt by someone in the group; they may change groups of friends. If the separation continues—even for a very short time—restoring that youth to the group's fellowship may become extremely difficult. Staying in contact with those who have withdrawn from your group is extremely important. At some point, each of these youth will have another need, and that need can be an opportunity to rebuild bridges between that person and the class.

Bonding is a serious part of any relationship. Keeping the relationship strong requires actions that demonstrate our care and concern. In Bible study classes, adult teachers and youth care leaders can play a vital role in maintaining contact and keeping the bonds strong among members and those who are being touched by the group.

What binds your Bible study group together? to your church? Describe some things your group does to bind each other together as a group.

What has caused some of your members not to feel bound to the group any longer? List some things that may have caused youth to pull away.

Community building brings balance and support to loving relationships. Jesus knew that His disciples would need one another as never before when He no longer could be with them. By His example, Jesus was putting into place simple communities. Wherever believers could gather together, there would be a new community of faith. Assimilating people into small groups for Bible study and service fits Jesus' example. Experience shows that those who are assimilated into smaller groupings are the ones who develop and grow as Christians. They are the ones who gain a sense of mission and purpose beyond themselves; this is extremely important to teens who often feel insecure and left out of things.

Each of us lives within various networks of people who represent for us varying types of community. Take the instance of Jesus healing the leper. No doubt word spread quickly throughout the leper network about how Jesus had healed the leper. Can you imagine what the leper must have told the other lepers about Jesus? "Here is a man who is willing to touch even us!" Are there adults and youth in your networks who need to be connected? Think about people in your Bible study group. What connections exist? Are there youth who are not connected? What are some things you can do to increase the bonds in your Bible study group?

Jealousy, or envy, is another factor that causes problems among believers. Throughout Scripture we are warned to avoid envy. The Old Testament contains stories of the jealousy between family members that led to deceit and even murder. Jealousy and envy are included in the lists of common vices throughout Paul's letters in the New Testament. In James 3:16, James wisely regarded envy as a source of disorder and evil practice. Christians may find themselves jealous of other believers who are receiving attention they themselves desire, or those who seem to receive more than their share of blessings. Envy disrupts loving relationships in the family of God in numerous ways.

In an interview of superstar tenors Jose Carreras, Placido Domingo, and Luciano Pavarotti, a reporter tried to emphasize the issue of competition between the three musicians. Instead, he received this reply from Domingo: "You have to put all of your concentration into opening your heart to the music. You can't be rivals when you're together making music."[2] These three men discovered the secret of relating without jealousy.

What do you most envy about others in your fellowship? Do you envy this trait or possession in all who possess it, or only in certain individuals? How does this envy separate you from others in the body of Christ?

Prejudice, common in the New Testament days, still causes separation among believers today. Jews hated Samaritans, considering them a mixed, impure race. Jesus took great care to set the example of the importance of relating to the Samaritans when He went through Samaria as He traveled from Judea to Galilee. An example of prejudicial behavior is evident when, upon hearing that Jesus was from Nazareth, Nathanael responded, "Can anything good come from there?" This attitude of prejudice expressed by a Canaanite about persons from a nearby town could have prevented Nathanael from meeting Jesus! Our prejudice prevents us from developing relationships with others, even other believers, as we prejudge them. Prejudice may manifest itself in many forms: racial, educational, economic, cultural, sexual, and so on. Prejudice exists anytime we allow differences (perceived or otherwise) to prevent interaction with others. Paul made a definitive statement against prejudice in Galatians 3:28: *There is neither Jew nor Greek, slave nor free, male nor female, for you are all one in Christ Jesus.* We act against the Word of God when we allow these differences to separate us. What a tragic occurrence in the body of Christ!

Pride is another trait that separates believers. Jesus told a parable of two men who prayed, describing a Pharisee who prayed about himself and the virtues he saw in himself, and a tax collector who humbly prayed for forgiveness from sins. The Pharisee was not really speaking to God, but telling those within earshot of his fine religious behavior. The tax collector, however, prayed to God with confession and an attitude of repentance. Jesus declared only the tax collector justified before God, for only those who humble themselves will be exalted. Pride has a tendency to blind us to our faults, and it can come in many forms: pride in abilities, in life experiences, financial attainment, culture, or race. Jesus denounced it, for it separates all people, even Christians.

Consider, instead, the path of humility, as portrayed by one participant in the 1994 Super Bowl loss of the Buffalo Bills to the Dallas Cowboys. Thurman Thomas, the Bills' star running back, sat on the Buffalo bench after the game, head bowed, with his hands covering his face. His three fumbles had contributed to his team's loss. Suddenly Emmitt Smith, the star running back of the Cowboys, stood before him. Smith had just been named Most Valuable Player for Super Bowl XXVIII. Holding his small goddaughter, he looked down at her and said, "I want you to meet the greatest running back in the NFL, Mr. Thurman Thomas."[3]

Consider the various types of pride and determine which is the most likely to be present in your life. Are there activities in the church in which you do not participate or individuals in the church to whom you do not relate because of pride? How does pride separate you from other believers in your church?

Which of the traits listed above (*an unforgiving spirit, jealousy, prejudice, and pride*) is most likely to separate you from other believers? Why?

The people of the early church experienced an incredible sense of community based on their knowledge of the risen Lord. They set a clear example of how believers should relate to one another with an attitude of servanthood. The Book of Acts, as well as the letters of the New Testament written by various apostles, tell believers today of the actions and attitudes of the early Christians. First of all, they were willing to pray with and for each other. Throughout the New Testament we are told of occasions of shared prayer—for an urgent need, such as an apostle who was imprisoned, or simply in the common practice of prayer. These early Christians also broke bread, or shared meals together, as detailed in Acts 2:42. They shared everything. They even sold their possessions as necessary to provide for the needs of others. They ministered to the sick and/or grieving; they spoke on behalf of other believers, as in the case of Paul who wrote a letter to Philemon, asking him to receive his slave who had stolen from him and run away, but later came to faith in Christ. These early Christians opened their homes to each other for prayer, sharing meals, and lengthier stays. They organized to meet needs in whatever way was necessary—they cared for widows and orphans. Reading the Book of Acts will bring to light the numerous ways those members of the early church served each other.

Consider the various acts of service among believers in the early church. Which of these ministries is best carried out in your church today? Which of them need to be better implemented in your local body of Christ?

Service is an action that tends to bind believers to each other. Where are the opportunities to serve your fellow believers? They're everywhere! Open your hearts and minds, along with your eyes, to discover them! Challenge yourself by carrying a blank sheet of paper with you as you go about the Sunday activities at your church. Jot down service and ministry ideas as you move among the various age groups. The following ideas have proven to be effective in various churches and may remind you of creative new ways to serve the believers in your local body of Christ.

• Consider a sixteen-year-old girl who became pregnant. A Christian and a church member, she occasionally attended Sunday School, but not on a regular basis. One of the girls in her class decided to give a maternity shower to provide necessary clothes for the mother-to-be. Invited to the shower were school friends, friends from church, and Sunday School workers. This servant-hearted teenager was criticized by some who felt she was "glorifying" the condition of teenage pregnancy outside of marriage. Had they opened their minds and hearts they would have realized she was trying to meet a need of someone in the body of Christ.

• A youth minister decided to use the elbow grease and energy of her teenagers when a family in the church was hospitalized after being involved in a serious car accident. There were no fatalities, but many bruises, cuts, and a multitude of broken bones. As Thanksgiving approached, the family realized they would be unable to prepare for the relatives that had previously planned to come for a visit. Then the teenagers took over! They secured permission to enter the family's home to clean house, change bedding, restock the refrigerator, and prepare for the guests' arrival. A youth group that is service-minded can be mobilized quickly to undertake such tasks!

• A mother of teenage girls realized the great need for a godly influence upon all the teenaged girls in her church. She organized a "For Young Ladies Only" luncheon in which she enlisted help from women in the girls. Many of the women involved were not mothers of teens, but chose to serve nonetheless. Each lady brought dishes (or, in some cases, paper plates) from home to decorate a table in her own unique theme. There was a guest speaker who challenged the girls to move beyond the cultural stereotype for girls in order to be who God created them to be. The girls were encouraged to begin watching these women to learn about the true model of femaleness which is neglected in the media today. The women were encouraged to begin relationships with the girls they met that day. Such relationships can be developed without a luncheon and guest speaker. A series of fellowship opportunities can accomplish the same goal. It is simply a matter of becoming more aware of the needs of teenage girls and focusing on meeting as many of the needs as possible.

• What about the school-aged children who stay late on Wednesday evening while parents are in choir rehearsal? You may secure one or two individuals to monitor a study hall in which assistance with homework or preparation for exams is provided. Older teens or adults could provide such a service. If transportation is provided, there are probably retired school teachers who would enjoy the opportunity to serve their church family in this way.

• A church family with senior adults is very blessed! Elderly people have many needs. These needs may be as simple as changing light bulbs or trimming shrubbery away from a window. A team could spend one Saturday morning each month meeting needs that have been turned in to the church office or one of the staff members. A team of one or two teenagers may deliver a tape and order of worship to those senior adults who cannot leave their home or nursing home to participate in worship services. Many deacon groups support "Senior Singles" ministries to those whose spouses have died. Teens may assist deacons in many of these tasks.

• Ask teens to serve at the fellowships, banquets, and other activities for those senior adults who are able to attend church activities. This principle may cross all age lines: Young adults may host a fellowship for median adults, teens may provide child care for preschoolers, and so forth.

• Many churches rely upon their members for lawn maintenance and landscaping. Consider asking Sunday School departments of various ages to adopt a task and accept responsibility for such tasks as mowing the lawn or maintaining the flower beds for a month. For churches who depend upon members for cleaning their building, the same plan can apply for building upkeep.

• An often-overlooked area of service is that of the greeter on Sunday morning. Instead of merely posting greeters at the entrances of the church buildings, ask for volunteers to be stationed at the parking areas to assist mothers with infants (and diaper bags!) and young children, as well as senior adults who need help carrying their Bibles, purses, or Sunday School books as they use their canes and/or walkers. Often, assistance is needed by those who are bringing refreshments or learning materials for the Sunday School classes. A helping hand can be provided by a person of almost any age and is always welcome in these situations!

• The electronic age in which we live provides other ways of service as church members can stay in touch through Email with missionaries on foreign fields. What about communication with those who are serving in the armed forces? Many people enjoy serving as encouragers by writing letters and making phone calls to others. We now have the ever-increasing challenge of maintaining contact with many children and teenagers who spend blocks of time with non-custodial parents or grandparents. Encouraging others is a well-received gift of service in God's family.

> Determine your *SQ* (service quotient) by responding to the following statements with *N* (never), *R* (rarely), *S* (sometimes), or *F* (frequently).
>
> 1.___I listen to the members of my Sunday School class to determine needs I might be able to meet.
>
> 2.___As I read the names of those in the hospital or the homebound, I follow up with a phone call to determine ways I can help.
>
> 3.___When I hear of a need in an area of the church where I do not generally serve, I still consider it my responsibility.
>
> 4.___I am as willing to work on the kitchen clean-up crew for an all-church dinner as to serve in a more high-profile position, such as leading in prayer, sharing a testimony, or providing music.
>
> 5.___I would rather write a check to meet a need than provide for it personally with my time and energy.
>
> 6.___I leave many of the tasks requiring manual labor for those who do not serve in the teaching ministries of the church as I do.
>
> 7.___As I grow older I believe I should be exempt from many areas of service in which I have already "served my time."

Scoring: For statements 1-4, give yourself 4 points for every F, 3 points for every S, 2 points for every R, 1 point for every N. For statements 5-7, give yourself 4 points for every N, 3 points for every R, 2 points for every S, 1 point for every F. The maximum (ideal) score is 28 points; the minimum score is 7 points. Evaluate the responses you gave. How can you improve your SQ?

The ideas for service in the body of Christ are as many and varied as the needs. No one can be available at all times to assist in every way. We can, however, organize into groups (such as Sunday School classes or mission action groups) to be available to meet certain needs. One person may decide to place his name on the list to assist on a monthly basis with light maintenance at the homes of the elderly, while another chooses to serve every two months as a parking lot attendant to help with needs there. A little organization goes a long way in preventing the burnout of a few willing persons. It also ensures the involvement of more members of the body of Christ.

As we consider undertaking such tasks we may ask ourselves, *Where will this lead? Do I have the time/energy/interest to keep up with a continuing stream of needs of other people? Is there a place I can 'draw the line' and withdraw from the situation?* There are no easy answers to these questions. It is truly an investment of time, energy, and interest to make oneself available to meet the needs of others—especially those needs within the body of Christ that are long-term needs, rather than one-time needs. We do not know where this involvement will lead or what it may demand from us physically or emotionally. Service to others makes us vulnerable as we open ourselves to the hurts and needs of those around us. It may be emotionally expensive at times. But, service is a primary way in which we can follow Christ's example of "being last," "being least," and being "servant of all."

Service to others is a privilege. Along with it come eternal rewards. The greatest reward of all, however, will be the commendation of our Savior when we meet Him face-to-face and He says, "Well done, good and faithful servant!"

stretching

Which of your attitudes needs to change in order for Christ to more completely use you to serve and love other Christians? What are you going to do to make these changes?

1. *Dallas Morning News*, Oct. 6, 1996, 11A.
2. *Leadership*, Spring 1996, 68. *The Atlantic Monthly*, 11/94
3. *Leadership*, Fall, 1994, 42.

chapter 4

Love Your Neighbor

I did not want to go through Samaria. I told Jesus that. I had never met a Samaritan I liked. In fact, I had never met one that I thought God liked. If there was one place that all of us disciples disagreed with Jesus, it was in this matter of loving Samaritans—those half-breed Jews! They weren't only mixed up in their blood lines, they were mixed up in their doctrine as well.

They had come into being after the Assyrian deportation of the Jews. Unfortunately some of them came back and intermarried with some of the local Canaanites. Still others of the Samaritans were the result of those few Jewish stragglers who married and hid out during the deportation. These Jews had beaten the returning exiles to the best farms of the land.

As I said, their doctrine was as offensive as their mixed blood. They believed—get this now—that Mt. Gerizim was the holy mountain of God. Now everybody who knows history knows that from the reign of King David onward the real mountain of God was Mt. Zion. But that's the way it was with Samaritans—they didn't allow sound doctrine to clutter up their minds. So they could just sanctify any common hill and call it the mountain of God.

Furthermore, Samaritans believed that when the messiah came he would just skip right over Zion and set up his temple on Mt. Gerizim. They even acted like they thought God was a Samaritan. They saw themselves as the chosen people. James and John once got so mad at some uppity Samaritans that they wanted to call down fire from heaven to fry the bigots. Jesus called Zebedee's boys "the Sons of Thunder" from that moment on.

When you think of how mixed up Samaritans were, you can understand why all good Jews avoided traveling through the hill country of Samaria. It made the trip a little longer, but we preferred to walk around the little principality than to go through it. But on this trip to Jerusalem, for some reason, Jesus said He had to go through Samaria.

We all wanted to ask why, but deep down we knew—He had to go through Samaria because He loved Samaritans. So we did it—we went right through Samaria with Jesus. We were really tired and hungry by the time we arrived at the little village of Sychar. It was hot, so we didn't smell all that good either. Seems I remember an old proverb that says, "A Jew never minds smelling bad in Samaria."

   Some of us decided we ought to go into town and try to buy some food. Our grub was running low because thirteen guys hiking in the mountains can eat their weight in dried fish pretty quickly. Jesus preferred to be left alone, so we left Him sitting by Jacob's Well while the rest of us went as a group into the little village to look for supplies. Frankly, any one of us would have been afraid to go alone. There was safety in numbers. As the old saying goes, "To a worm in horseradish the whole world is horseradish." That's how we felt in Sychar. To a Jew in Samaria the whole world was Samaritans.

   The next part of this story happened while we were in Sychar. We hadn't been gone long when a Samaritan woman came alone to the well to draw water. When any woman goes to the well alone, right off you know she's a lonely woman. Drawing water is a social event in every town. Sometimes women liked to go to the well together just so they could talk freely. This woman was likely one of the people the other women freely talked about.

   When the woman reached the well, Jesus asked her for a drink. She was stunned! He was a Jew; she was a Samaritan. While none of the Samaritans had ever won medals for good behavior, Jesus later told a story about one good Samaritan. Most Jews felt that a reference to a "good Samaritan" was an oxymoron. Well this woman was what even the bad Samaritans called a "bad Samaritan." People who cared what others thought about them avoided her.

   "Hello! How about a drink?" asked Jesus.

   "Whoa there! Does this look like a Jewish well to you? There may be places where Jews are in the majority, but this isn't it. Excuse me, but I'll get my water and go. The Jews have no dealings with the Samaritans."

   "Too bad! If you only knew Who I am, you could have asked Me for a drink of a kind of water not available at this well—living water."

   "Really, where's your water pot and well rope? The water in this well is too deep to reach without a jar and rope." She smirked. (Had the Sons of Thunder been there, they probably would have thrown her in the well.) She lifted her chin, tossed her head with an air of arrogance, and said, "Are you greater than our father Jacob who gave us this well? Surely I don't need to remind a Jew of how Jacob brought this water to us more than a thousand years ago. Yet he never called it living water."

   "Nonetheless," Jesus continued, "everyone who drinks of this water will be thirsty again, but whoever drinks the water I give will never thirst. Indeed this water will be like a spring of water, welling up into eternal life."

"I'll take a jug of that right now!" she declared rather pointedly.

"Well then, go call your husband and come back," said Jesus.

"I'll have you know I have no husband," said the woman as she pulled the well rope casually back to the surface. She cocked her head as if to give the impression that she had nothing to hide. Her actions seemed to imply that while many men had tried to win her affections none had managed to do so. She wanted to appear as pure as the white snows of Mt.Hermon."No, no. I don't have a husband" she repeated. She took her water pot and started to walk away.

"You're right about that," Jesus called after her. "At the moment you have no husband, but you had five before your last divorce."

She dropped the clay jar.

"And furthermore the man you're living with now is not your husband."

The woman turned back to Him in amazement. "Sir, I see you are a prophet!" she exclaimed.

Once her past was uncovered, she tried to recover her own self-esteem with compliments and theology. The compliment came first. "Sir, I see you are able to read minds and know the thoughts of complete strangers like myself." Jesus would not be distracted by shallow words of praise.

She quickly moved to theology. "You know many people believe that one religion is rather like another. You Jews say Mt. Zion is God's favorite temple site, and we say it's Mt. Gerizim. Won't it be wonderful when people of all religions join hands and walk along together? But tell me. Do you think God's mountain is our mountain or yours?"

Jesus thought a moment and went on. "Believe me, woman, the time is coming when you will worship the Father neither on this mountain nor in Jerusalem. You Samaritans worship what you do not know; we Jews worship what we do know, for salvation has always been the agenda of the Jews. It has always been our calling to reveal salvation to the world. Salvation has always been from the Jews. A time is coming and is now here when all true worshippers will worship the Father in Spirit and in truth, for these are the kind of worshippers the Father seeks. God is Spirit and His worshippers must worship Him in Spirit and in truth."

The woman knew she had been outflanked by someone of great mind and heart. She could neither defend her poor morality or her lost self-esteem, still she struggled to have the last word. "OK. We all know when the Messiah comes, He will explain everything to us all, even us Samaritans."

"I am He," said Jesus.

The woman's jaw dropped. Her world seemed to stop. She looked stupefied. She could say nothing more.

About this time all of us came back from town. To be honest, we were surprised to see Jesus talking to the Samaritan woman. Clearly, she was not the kind of woman the Messiah talked to if He wanted to keep His messianic reputation.

We all watched the woman as she left her water jar and hurried away. Back in Sychar, she ran to all her acquaintances, shouting, "Come see a man who told me everything I ever did!"

Everything? some of her neighbors wondered. Since she was an experienced woman, she had their instant attention. By the scores they all began following her out of the little town back to where we were.

Meantime at the well, Jesus refused to eat the food we had secured in the village. He said, "I have food to eat that you do not know." We wondered if someone had already brought Him something while we were away.

"No," said Jesus. "My food is to do the will of Him who sent me and to complete all that He has asked me to do. Do not say there are still four months to harvest. Open your eyes and look on the fields, they are ripe already to harvest.

"Even now, the reaper draws his wages. Even now he harvests the crop of eternity. So now the sower and the reaper can rejoice together. Even as we rejoice the old proverb has come true: one sows and another reaps. I sent you to reap what you've never worked for. Others have done the hard work, and you have reaped the benefits of their labor."

Here in the hot, arid hill country of Samaria, a vision began to settle down on us even as Jesus talked. He finished His private discourse to us just as the Samaritans arrived at the well. *Open your eyes. Look on the fields. They are ready for harvest.* Those words took on a gripping new meaning.

The woman herself was the first one back to Jesus. She fell at His feet and began to weep. Between her tears she cried out, "I openly confess. I surrender my phony self-esteem. I surrender my braggadocio. I give up my immoral lies to protect my immoral past. Give me your living water that I may be forever free of every thirst."

The woman was all tears, and yet all joy. Her confession had bathed her in new honesty. She pointed to Jesus and shouted to the people of Sychar, "Here He is! The Christ! Believe with me."

Many began to elbow their way through the crowd toward Jesus. They, too, fell on their faces and their tears of joy ran more freely than the water of Jacob's well. They cried to the woman, "We no longer believe because of your testimony. No. No. Grace has washed our own eyes. It is easy to see that this is the Messiah, the Savior of the world."

In the distance I noticed the green wheat just thickening, waving like a thousand banners from above. Yes, I thought to myself. Jesus was right. It was not four months till harvest. I looked at kneeling men and women caught up in a new honesty, confessing old sins and life-long injustices. The harvest is now.

These joyous new converts invited us into their little town. We went. More preaching; more psalms of joy; more wonderful times with the Lord of the harvest! Over the next few days God was to teach me the real joy of it all. Jews and Samaritans had become one. Sinners had become friends.

Later we left Sychar and traveled on down toward Jerusalem. I felt only wonder. The wheat was growing. The harvest is now. Who would be the harvesters?

Love Your Neighbor

The Sunday School department of ninth and tenth graders had heard the story countless times before. As a matter of fact, it was one of the first stories a child hears at church. As the teachers met in their weekly planning meeting, they asked, "How can we make this story come alive in a fresh, new way?" They were discussing Jesus' parable of The Good Samaritan.

The account (found in Luke 10:25-37) begins with a scribe, or expert in the law, asking Jesus how he can inherit eternal life. The purpose of the question was to show Jesus as inadequate to answer such a theological question. The man went on to show his knowledge of the law by quoting Deuteronomy and Leviticus, concerning loving God with all of one's soul, strength, and mind, and loving one's neighbor as oneself. After Jesus affirmed the scribe's correct knowledge, the man asked one more question, *Who is my neighbor?* The man asking the question knew that for God love has no limits, but he was seeking to limit love for one's neighbor by the definition of *neighbor*. Jesus' answer to the question caused great discussion among the people of that time. Jesus answered with this parable:

There was a man who was going down the road from Jerusalem to Jericho; he was victimized by robbers and left for dead. We know nothing about the man—there is no racial, cultural, or physical description. The first person to come upon the victim was a priest who had completed his service in the Temple. Because he was a religious person, the priest probably asked himself many questions to determine his actions to the wounded man: *What if I touch him, discover he is dead, and become defiled? What if the man turns out to be someone who is not, according to my definition of the law, a neighbor?* His considerations made it easy to pass by the wounded man, walking "on the other side," or as far away from him as possible. The next traveler was a Levite, one of the helpers in the Temple. He behaved much the same way as the priest, and for the same reasons. The first two travelers missed the opportunity to serve their fellow man as they acted upon their limited understanding of the law.

The third traveler was a Samaritan. *Samaritan!* The very word brought deep feelings of prejudice from Jesus' listeners. Jews hated Samaritans! But, the Samaritan responded to the wounded man with an active love. He bandaged his wounds, applied oil and wine, placed the man on his own donkey, and took the man to an inn for care. This good Samaritan even made arrangements for the future care of the wounded man, pledging to pay the innkeeper for any expense incurred in caring for the man's needs.

Jesus then asked the question that drove to the point of the parable: Which of these three do you think was a neighbor to the man who fell into the hands of robbers? The scribe, knowing the correct answer, could not bring himself to say the word *Samaritan*. Instead, he said the one who had mercy on the man was the neighbor. Jesus' response was brief: *Go and do likewise*. In the Greek text, the personal pronoun is included: *You* do likewise. The point of this parable is clear—a neighbor is any other human being. There are no qualifications of race, religion, culture, or family background. Love for God demands that we love our neighbors.

Back to the Sunday School department of ninth and tenth graders. How did the Sunday School teachers solve their dilemma of how to teach this familiar story? They assigned a different setting to each group. One group portrayed the story as it might have happened in the "wild west;" another portrayed it in modern style; and another in true biblical fashion. Still another presented it as a case in court. Each group had to stay true to the principles of the account found in Luke 10. After each group made its presentation, the question was asked, "Who is my neighbor?" The answer was the same in each case—whether biblical, western, or modern day: Every human being is my neighbor!

A second applicable passage, found in Matthew 25:34-46, reveals God's criteria for inheriting His kingdom. Jesus told of those who are blessed by His Father. They are the ones whose actions evidenced their faith and love. The King in the story was hungry, thirsty, a stranger, needing clothes, sick, and in prison. The righteous ministered to Him, though they did not understand they were actually ministering to Christ. They did not undertake such actions in order to gain a reward, but because they saw another human being in need. The King responded, *I tell you the truth, whatever you did for one of the least of these brothers of mine, you did for me*. All those who did not respond in love to the people in need were taken away to eternal punishment. Some people may minister to the needs of others out of selfish motives. God, however, knows our hearts—He knows which actions reflect the inner nature of a person.

The story recorded in John 4 provides the example of Christ in a situation His disciples would have chosen to avoid. Jews did not travel through Samaria, but went around the country. Jews hated Samaritans, for they were a mixed race resulting from the marriage of Jews with non-Jews. Jesus purposefully chose to go through Samaria to meet the needs of those who lived there. His disciples needed to see firsthand the necessity of ministry among Samaritans. The incident with the woman at the well took place at the sixth hour (or around noon, according to Jewish time which is determined from sunrise to sunset). It is possible that the woman's poor reputation made it necessary for her to get water at a time when there were no crowds. Jesus' encounter with this woman is one that crosses the boundaries placed by people of that day and time, many of which prevail today. He (a Jew) ministered to someone who was considered unclean (a Samaritan). Jesus, in radical fashion, asked the woman for a drink of water. This request was shocking because Jews never shared food containers and utensils with Samaritans for fear of contamination. Not only was this woman a Samaritan, but she had a bad reputation for her past marital actions and her present situation of living with a man who was not her husband.

Through His conversation with her, Jesus offered the gift of living water, the same gift He offers to each of us. When Christ interacted with a person, He did not see race, culture, or background. He saw human beings in need of His saving touch. His world included everyone.

Consider the group of 25 teenagers returning from their mission trip to an inner city area. Before this mission experience, Holly was always more concerned with her own clothing, hair, and makeup than the needs of others. After the first day of Backyard Bible Clubs, she found herself with dirty children sitting in her lap with their arms around her neck. Dirty handprints covered her clothing where the children repeatedly touched her.

• Luis was "too cool" to be affected by the needs of others until he went to the rundown home of a little boy with AIDS. He previously had thought that people with AIDS were "getting what they deserved" until that first visit during which he could hardly remain in the home without breaking into tears. Each day thereafter he returned to spend time with the sick child.

• Robert had the attitude that everyone in the United States should be fluent in English and, if they weren't, it was their problem, not his. However, after one afternoon when trying to communicate the gospel to a non-English-speaking teenager, he became determined to learn the basics of his new friend's language. He also became active in "English as a second language" courses offered at a mission center when he returned home.

• One of the group's sponsors, Andy, did not have much sympathy for the unemployed; he felt that anyone who wanted a job could get a job. Then he met the mother of four children under the age of seven,. Her husband had deserted the family. She was torn between accepting a minimum wage job and staying home to care for her children. Andy exchanged his critical attitude for the question, "How can I help you?" Generally it takes only a limited amount of experience in a world that differs from the one in which we live each day to open the eyes of our hearts to the needs of others.

> How big is your world? In the space before the group description, place the appropriate letter to designate the frequency of your interaction with members of the particular group. F = Frequently, S = Sometimes, R = Rarely, N = Never.
>
> ___homeless
> ___physically disabled
> ___mentally disabled
> ___orphans
> ___economically disadvantaged
> ___AIDS patients
> ___non-English speaking
> ___those with a crisis pregnancy
> ___those of a different race/ethnic group
> ___chronically ill
> ___senior adults
> ___legal offenders
> ___illiterate
> ___abuse victims
> ___hospitalized
> ___homebound
> ___unemployed

SCRIPTURE PASSAGE	WHAT HAPPENED	HOW JESUS LOVED HIS NEIGHBOR
Mark 1:40-42	Jesus heals a man with leprosy.	
Mark 2:15-17	Jesus eats with sinners at the home of Matthew.	
Matthew 14:13-21	Jesus feeds the five thousand.	
Luke 7:36-50	Jesus responds to the sinful woman who anointed His feet.	
Luke 13:10-17	Jesus heals a crippled woman on the Sabbath.	
John 2:1-11	Jesus turns the water into wine.	
Luke 19:1-9	Jesus shares real life with Zacchaeus.	
John 8:1-11	Jesus forgives the woman caught in the act of adultery.	

Our basic beliefs as Christians lay the groundwork for our responsibility to other people. Consider these four belief statements:

1. God's grace and love extend to the entire world, not just to those who love Him. Our ministry efforts to others should mirror His concerns; His love is our model. If we love only those who love us, we are no different than the tax collectors!

2. Man was created in God's image and is, therefore, valuable. We are the highest achievement in God's creation. Belief in this statement has extensive theological implications! As descendants of Adam and Eve, we are all brothers, and we have responsibility for the welfare of others. No man is worthless according to God, who sent His Son to save mankind.

3. All human beings have sinned. We must be careful not to set ourselves above those who may have committed more "obvious" sins or sins in a different "category" than our own. Our refusal to help others is also a sin.

4. Jesus came to earth to save man. He set the example of meeting needs during His brief ministry on earth. Jesus identified with all human needs as He took on the nature of man. We are to minister in the same way.

If we accept the four belief statements listed above, we must act upon them. This love is what we must attempt to show every human being with whom we come in contact.

What might prevent people from being willing to meet the needs of their neighbors? One hindrance is lack of concern. Like many of the preceding examples, we might feel that the needy persons have caused their own problems and, therefore, they do not deserve the help of others. Another problem is our busyness. We do not make the time in our schedules of work, church activities, social activities, and the activities of our children, to meet the needs of those around us. Often we feel overwhelmed in the face of so many serious needs, we feel we can't really make a difference. We don't even know where to start! Even so, we must remember we can make a difference in the situations of one or two persons. We can obtain information on how to better meet these needs if we ask resource persons in our community who have worked with the particular ministry groups we are considering.

A major fulfillment of Jesus' commandment to love our neighbor is accomplished as we go about our daily lives. Because these opportunities are unscheduled and unexpected, we tend to neglect them due to their inconvenience or intrusiveness into our busy lifestyles. There are safety considerations, also: *Is it safe to lower a car window to assess a situation in which it appears help is needed?* There are also integrity questions: *Will this person use the money I give him to buy alcohol or drugs instead of food for the family?* It is not always easy to determine the best fulfillment of Jesus' commandment to love our neighbors.

Read the following case studies based on real-life situations. Choose the letter before the statement which, in your opinion, is the best way to love one's neighbor. You may want to suggest an idea that you feel is a better way to love as Christ would love.

1. A pastor is en route to Sunday services when he sees a woman with three small children standing beside a car with a flat tire on the side of the road. He should:

   a. Stop and give assistance, even if he is late for his obligations at church and possibly slightly greasy!

   b. Stop at the first available phone and call for assistance for the lady.

   c. Go on to church, and send someone to assist the lady.

   d. other_____

2. Betsy is busy decorating the school cafeteria for the band banquet when the twelve-year-old daughter of one of the school custodians approaches her. The young girl asks a question about the T-shirt Betsy is wearing with the logo of their summer youth camp. Betsy is in a hurry to finish her decorating so she can pick up her mom at work in 15 minutes. Betsy should:

   a. take time to chat with the girl, hoping it will lead to an opportunity to witness

   b. answer the girl's question, but kindly explain she cannot talk to her now because she is in a hurry to finish her work and pick up her mother

   c. answer the girl's question, explain that she cannot talk right then, but get the girl's address and phone number so she can make a personal visit later

   d. other_____

3. Traci, an eighth grader, discovers the man who has driven her school bus for the past few years is in the hospital. She knows very little about him or his family. The only time she ever sees him is on the school bus, but she feels they have become friends. She does not have his address or phone number. Traci should:

   a. send a card to the school district, hoping he will receive it

   b. do nothing, for it could be awkward trying to contact him since she knows nothing about him or his family

   c. call the school district to find out where he is in the hospital and go visit him with several other youth from his bus route.

   d. other_____

4. On a cold winter night, a lawyer is making a late evening delivery to a jailer at the courthouse. He sees the familiar face of a street person at the courthouse door. The man is hungry and is asking for money for food. The lawyer should:

   a. give the man money so he can buy food at a nearby fast-food restaurant

   b. get the man some food and bring it back to him

   c. offer to take the man to get something to eat

   d. other_____

In many cases, showing love for one's neighbor is not a spontaneous action. Often, planning is required to determine and carry out the most effective ways to show this love. We may undertake an ongoing ministry to those in need, or consider a one-time project. How do we mobilize our resources, particularly in the area of youth ministry, to undertake a project that shows love to our neighbors? Our Acteens, Royal Ambassador Pioneers, and High School Baptist Young Men spend a great deal of time and energy in planning such events.

Denominational agencies, such as the North American and International Mission Boards, as well as State Conventions, local associations, and independent benevolent groups, can provide ideas for mission tasks. These organizations provide excellent resources in this area. *The Acteen Leader Manual* gives eight basic suggestions for organizing and carrying out Acteens mission action. These suggestions, in slightly modified form, apply to all of us:

Step 1: Discover Needs—Youth may know of situations in the community where they can provide assistance. Mission organizations in the church, as well as staff members, have a good idea of the needs in the area. Other needs may develop as a result of crisis—such as flood, tornado, drought, or war.

Step 2: Choose Which Need to Meet—It is impossible to respond to every need your youth might want to address. Choose a need youth can understand and meet.

Step 3: Determine a Project—Carefully consider various aspects of the project before you choose it. Will you be able to complete the project? Is another group in your community already meeting the need? Do you have the resources in time, money, and skills to carry out the project?

Step 4: Plan the Project—Answer the basic questions, *Who? What? When? Where? How much? What training is necessary?*

Step 5: Enlist Youth and Adults—Some youth and adults who are not the leaders in other areas of the youth ministry in your church may be willing to get involved in a mission project . Don't overlook them!

Step 6: Train Youth and Adults—This is an absolute necessity. Proper training increases confidence among the youth and adults involved.

Step 7: Carry Out the Project—Do what you have planned and trained to do!

Step 8: Evaluate the Project—Don't neglect this step! Allow both youth and adults, as well as any contact persons representing the recipients of the mission action, to evaluate the project. Ask: Did we accomplish our purpose? Were we adequately prepared and trained? Did we deal properly with any problems we encountered? How can we improve?

Refer to the response sheet, "Ideas for Ministry." Listed below are some specific ideas for ministry to each of the ten groups on the sheet. This listing will undoubtedly remind you of many more ways you can meet the needs of these neighbors.

Physically Disabled Persons
- Provide transportation
- Run errands
- Provide needed equipment, such as crutches or wheelchairs
- Read to them
- Help with personal grooming (hair, nails)
- Write letters for them

Mentally Disabled Persons
- Visit the person to allow time out for their caregivers
- Provide music activities
- Give parties
- Provide recreational activities
- Provide activities outside the home

Senior Adults
- Provide meals
- Take pets to visit them, if appropriate
- Phone them often to check on them and to determine needs
- Provide items they need, such as stamps, night lights, body lotion
- Send cards and letters

Economically Disadvantaged Persons
- Provide clothing
- Provide personal toiletries, such as soap, toothbrush, toothpaste, or shampoo
- Provide fruit
- Provide baby formula, baby food, diapers
- Help repair or paint home

Illiterate Persons
- Provide taped reading material and a cassette recorder
- Make or purchase educational material needed by those who teach them to read
- Provide child care during teaching sessions
- Provide reading material at the appropriate level
- Provide tutoring for them and their children

Internationals
- Invite them to your home for a meal and fellowship
- Help them learn English
- Remember their ethnic holidays
- Distribute Bibles and study material in their language
- Acquaint them with your city, its stores, medical services, cultural opportunities, and so on

Chronically Ill
- Listen; visit with them
- Provide assistance with chores at their home
- Sit with them to allow time off for caregivers
- Take balloons, flowers, and/or pictures children have drawn
- Send cards and letters

Legal Offenders
- Provide Christian reading material
- Arrange transportation for family, if needed
- Write letters
- Mentor, tutor, or hire a youth on probation
- Provide recreational activities

Victims of Natural Disaster
- Provide food, shelter and clothing (and necessary care for the clothing)
- Provide transportation
- Provide child care
- Help secure medical care, legal assistance, assistance with insurance claims, and so on
- Provide school supplies or educational needs for children

Families in Other Stressful Situations
- Be a friend
- Help secure legal assistance or counseling

- Provide child care
- In abuse situations, help secure emergency housing
- In crisis pregnancy, provide maternity clothing and help secure prenatal medical care

One particular group of neighbors is represented in more than one of the ministry groups listed above. They have special needs that are unique to many of the neighbors we often encounter. These special needs include: mental retardation, visual impairment, learning disability, gifted, physical disability, deaf/hearing impairment. If we are seeking to love our neighbors, we will be loving and ministering to many individuals with special needs. As we minister to these individuals, we may need to develop new skills (such as sign language), obtain health information (such as a basic understanding of their physical problems, when to assist and not to assist a disabled person, and skill in administering CPR), and practice new techniques (such as how to develop extra patience with an attention deficient teen). Volunteers at a development center for mentally retarded adults found it difficult to accept the residents' great need to touch them, hug them, and hold their hands. They later came to realize how Jesus ministered through His loving touch. Touching was a way they could meet the needs of these very special neighbors! Too long we have overlooked the needs of these individuals, both in our ministry opportunities outside the church and our programming inside the church. Jesus never overlooked them! If we are to follow Christ's example, we, too, must become aware of their many needs and determine how we can meet them.

Whenever we reach out to love our neighbors, there are hazards involved. We do not know where our involvement will lead. We may be rejected. We may even regret becoming involved because of the actions or reactions of those we try to help. In some cases, the people we help may want us to become involved in other aspects of their lives in which we may not feel adequate or comfortable.

Occasionally, those we have helped may want to visit our churches. Do we have confidence in the manner in which our fellow Christians would respond if these neighbors visited our Sunday School classes and our sanctuaries?

One youth minister told of a group of unchurched teenagers to whom he was seeking to minister. On a Sunday evening, they decided to visit his church. The group entered the balcony area and located places to sit. They promptly began eating the snacks and drinking the cold drinks they had brought with them, while resting their feet on the chairs in front of them. They had not visited a worship service before. They did not know the standard of behavior was not like that at a movie theatre. How would your church members respond to those unreached and unchurched youth?

In her book pertaining to lifestyle evangelism, *Out of the Saltshaker*, Rebecca Manley Pippert tells the poignant story of a college student in Portland, Oregon.[2] His hair was never combed and—regardless of the weather—he was barefoot. He was a brilliant student who had become a

Christian while in college. One day he decided to attend a traditional, middle-class church across the street from his campus that was trying to develop a ministry to college students.

He walked into this church, wearing his blue jeans, tee shirt, and of course no shoes. People looked a bit uncomfortable, but no one said anything. So Bill began walking down the aisle looking for a seat. The church was quite crowded that Sunday, so as he got down to the front pew and realized that there were no seats, he just squatted on the carpet--perfectly acceptable behavior at a college fellowship, but perhaps unnerving for a church congregation. The tension in the air became so thick one could slice it.

Suddenly an elderly man began walking down the aisle toward the boy. Was he going to scold Bill? My friends who saw him approaching said they thought, *You can't blame him. He'd never guess Bill is a Christian. And his world is too distant from Bill's to understand. You can't blame him for what he's going to do.*

As the man kept walking slowly down the aisle, the church became utterly silent, all eyes were focused on him; you could not hear anyone breathe. When the man reached Bill, with some difficulty he lowered himself and sat down next to him on the carpet. He and Bill worshiped together on the floor that Sunday. I was told there was not a dry eye in the congregation!

Bill's experience happened the way we would wish anyone's experience with Christians would unfold. Though the neighbor in this story was already a believer, that fact was unknown as the drama unfolded. The response of the elderly man tends to amaze us because of his willingness to love this unknown and untraditionally-attired neighbor. He was willing to leave his comfort zone and risk the disapproval of his fellow Christians to reach out to him in the sanctuary of his church. Loving one's neighbor should be easier in our churches; but, unfortunately, it is sometimes harder.

List the types of people against whom you are likely to feel prejudice. Why do you feel the way you do? Is it a result of negative experience, tradition, or ignorance? How does prejudice separate you from others in the body of Christ?

Becoming a friend to someone outside our group requires intentional effort from us. We must be willing to go the greater distance and meet them more than halfway. We may need to learn more about their beliefs, values, customs, and hopes if we are to become friends with people who are not part of our usual circle of friends, people we might describe as "not like us." Bridging cultural barriers is a challenge. Interestingly, cultural barriers often exist between people in our own communities. We need go no farther than our own communities to find them.

If you live in an urban, suburban, or small community environment, identify an area that might include your apartment building, subdivision, or five or six nearby blocks; list the various cultural, economic, or lifestyle groups represented in the people who live near you. If you are in a rural setting, think of the people who live in a radius of a few miles. Think carefully and see how many variations you can list. Write names of people who come to mind

Love requires unconditional acceptance of people as individuals. Opportunities for grace abound in such a climate. Attitude is everything. People are people and share common needs, hopes, and aspirations. Christ's focus stayed on people rather than social classes. He saw their need and responded to it. He shared in their common humanity and helped them accept God's uncommon love.

We face many barriers in fulfilling Christ's commission to take the gospel to all people. Prejudice may be the most difficult of all barriers to overcome. Prejudice has deep roots in most of our cultures. Whether or not we acknowledge it, prejudice is firmly rooted in our experience, regardless of what culture we are a part. In a thousand subtle ways, we live out the teachings and prejudices with which we grew up. Overcoming prejudice begins with getting close enough to see others as they really are and not as we assume them to be.

List some ways that can help you get around the barriers. What are they?

Consider such things as prayer, developing the habit of meeting people, doing deeds of kindness to build bridges, starting a Bible study group, conduct a ministry project, make contact with one person and get to know that one person for no other reason than you are interested in him or her.

Select one action to take. Pray about the action and respond to the doors that God opens for you to do that or a similar action.

Are we willing to take the necessary risks in order to love our neighbors? Can we accept ridicule and criticism from others, as well as deal with our own fears? Are we willing to suffer disappointment and rejection? Are we willing to put hands and feet to our faith or does it have only words? Jesus commands unselfish love for all people. This love must be given without regard for the merit of the recipient. Christ's love must be evident in every aspect of our lives. As Christians we must come to the point of honest self-examination. It is the choice of each individual believer whether or not to obey our Lord's teaching. Our decision today must be whether or not we will obey Jesus' brief, yet clear, command: *Go and do likewise.*

stretching

Who are the people outside of your comfort zone—those you have "passed by on the other side" in the past? How do you plan to respond to them now? To what ministry groups will you find ways to show Christ's love and meet needs?

IDEAS FOR MINISTRY

Who are the groups to whom we need to minister? Below are ten ministry groups representing various needs in our society. Write a physical or material need members of this group might have, a difficulty or problem they might have, and one word to describe a person in this ministry group. The first group has been completed as an example.

1. PHYSICALLY DISABLED PERSONS
    Difficulty/problem: Transportation
    One-word description: Immobile
    Physical/material need: Wheelchairs
2. MENTALLY DISABLED PERSONS
    Difficulty/problem:
    One-word description:
    Physical/material need:
3. SENIOR ADULTS
    Difficulty/problem:
    One-word description:
    Physical/material need:
4. ECONOMICALLY DISADVANTAGED PERSONS
    Difficulty/problem:
    One-word description:
    Physical/material need:
5. ILLITERATE PERSONS
    Difficulty/problem:
    One-word description:
    Physical/material need:
6. INTERNATIONALS
    Difficulty/problem:
    One-word description:
    Physical/material need:
7. CHRONICALLY ILL PERSONS
    Difficulty/problem:
    One-word description:
    Physical/material need:
8. LEGAL OFFENDERS
    Difficulty/problem:
    One-word description:
    Physical/material need
9. VICTIMS OF NATURAL DISASTER
    Difficulty/problem:
    One-word description:
    Physical/material need:
10. FAMILIES IN OTHER DIFFICULT SITUATIONS
    Difficulty/problem:
    One-word description:
    Physical/material need:

By naming specific groups and jotting down some of their specific needs and problems, we are able to better consider how we might go about meeting their needs.

[1]. Marti Soloman, *Acteens Leader Manual* (Birmingham, AL, Woman's Missionary Union, 1988), 52-54.
[2]. Rebecca Manley Pippert, *Out Of The Saltshaker* (Downer's Grove, Ill: Intervarsity Press, 1979), 177-78

chapter 5

I Am Sending You

I must confess that the resurrection made all of us nervous. The Risen Lord was prone to show up in the most unlikely places. For instance, once in a sealed room He came like an explosion of light in our midst. Another time He appeared suddenly like a phantom, but immediately took on what to us was solid form.

If His unannounced appearances made me edgy, they were nearly impossible for Thomas. Thomas was not with the rest of us when the Lord first appeared. When we told him we had seen Jesus alive, he blurted out, "Hey guys, get honest! Unless I can stick my fingers into the print of the nails and thrust my hand into His wounded side, I will not believe. Jesus is dead . . . dead . . . dead. Wake up! Face it! Do you hear me?"

So Thomas went another full week in raging doubt. The following Sunday Jesus once again suddenly appeared before us. Jesus, knowing somehow about Thomas' noisy doubts, invited him to stick his fingers in His injured hands and side. Thomas got honest. He fell down and said, "My Lord and God!"

After that, Jesus continued appearing in and out of our lives. Then for a period of time we didn't see Him. I really started getting nervous. We all began to wonder if He had left forever. We didn't know what to do. I personally began to feel an urge to return to the sea. Jesus still had given us no clear instructions on whether or how we were to start His kingdom.

Galilee loomed large in my mind for the first time in a long time. I remembered how beautiful it was. The lapping waves, all night fishing trips, the golden sunrises, and heading home with a whole boat full of silver fish. The longer I meditated the more I felt the yen to return to the sea. It seemed to me the kingdom of God was over.

"I'm going fishing!"

The others were dumfounded at my words.

"Anybody want to go?"

Six of the other disciples who were with me at the time agreed to go. The old boats and nets were pretty dry. We took awhile to get things ready, for it had been a long time since any of us had gone on a real fishing trip. Nevertheless, before long the seven of us put out to sea. We were still confused about the kingdom, but out there on the sea all was peaceful.

The truth was, however, we didn't really want to be fishing. We wanted to be with Jesus, like we had once been. We wanted to be walking along the lanes of Jerusalem and sleeping and talking late with the Master under the open sky. Where was He?

We sailed all night on Galilee. It was a bad night for fishing. We caught nothing! We kept throwing out our nets but always the same thing—nothing! Nothing also was what we were without Jesus.

"Isn't this fun?" asked John, the teenager. "I wish I hadn't come!"

I was thinking the same thing—about him and me. It was a miserable, unrewarding night. We were worn out and frustrated. Our backs were breaking. Moreover, our inner resentments were all pretty near the surface. Why were we out here in the first place? What had happened to the kingdom of God? Where was Jesus?

I threw a net out one more useless time. Even before the wet cords hit the water, I wished I was home by the fire permanently. What had happened? "Jesus," rebuking Him for His absence, "Where are You? Don't you care if we're out here on Galilee, trying to feel good about ourselves but unable to catch a thing? It was You who filled us with all of these dreams of changing our world. Now we're out here all alone and You're somewhere else. We've fished all night and caught nothing. We've been catching a lot of that lately." (*Nothing* is what you catch most when you are powerless and all alone.)

"Hey out there, have you caught any fish?" Someone from the shore was calling out across the grey sea. I wanted to say, "What's it to you?" But I answered more civilly, "No. Nothing." *Nothing* was the word for the day.

"Well, let down your nets on the starboard side," the man called.

Such an idiotic suggestion! It made me mad. "Oh sure." I muttered. "What a brilliant suggestion. If at first you try and don't succeed off the port side, try the starboard side. That must be why we've caught nothing. The fish are all on the other side of the boat. Hey, Andrew, the fish are all on the other side! That guy on the shore says we've been fishing off the wrong side. Can you believe that?" We laughed like adolescents at the idea.

You know, I'm not sure why we did it, but we lugged all those soggy seines across the boat one more time. We threw 'em as far out as we could. Then we started trying to pull 'em back. We couldn't; they wouldn't come. "We must have snagged something on the bottom of the lake," said John.

As we tugged on the wet nets, I began to see the roll and turn of churning silver in the nets. "Shiloh and Sinai, Andrew," I called. "We've got fish! Look at this!"

Andrew's mouth gaped. His jaw fell down over his Adam's apple. Andrew was not a handsome brother even when he wasn't surprised. Was he ever surprised now! All of us were.

"Hey, you guys, help us!" I cried out to the others. As we pulled the nets toward the boat, we could see the silver flash of white bellies and green fins. They were churning with anger, trying to escape. I prayed a little selfishly that the nets wouldn't break. Soon we had the fish alongside the boat. Man these fish were big!

"Shall we try to get 'em in the boat, Peter, or just tug 'em alongside? We're less than 150 yards off shore," said Andrew.

"It's the Lord!" cried John.

John jumped out of the boat and thrashed the water, swimming, then running toward the shore. He was young and moved fast. I had been fishing nearly naked. We often did when the weather was warm and the work was hard. This kept us from sweating through our good clothes. But it was good to see Jesus! Suddenly the glory of the moment overwhelmed me! I put on my robe and jumped over the edge of the boat and ran to Him.

When we got to Capernaum Beach, Jesus had a hot bed of embers with fish frying. Bread, hot and inviting, toasted at the edge of the fire.

The terrible feelings of abandonment that had come over us during the night, melted away and were replaced with instant joy. I felt so great in Jesus' presence. I had a great reluctance to move. I was afraid that if I did move, the delicious spectre of His reality would evaporate.

I so wanted to say, "Jesus, please don't leave us again. Please don't make us wonder where you are to the extent that we no longer know who we are. Please don't make us go back to fishing." I didn't really say any of those things; I just thought them. My thoughts were interrupted by the realization that Jesus was speaking to me.

"It's time for some more fish. Bring some of the fish you just caught."

"Yes sir!" I said cheerfully.

I ran back to the boat and dragged the net back upon the shore. These were big fish! And lots of them too. "Andrew," I yelled. "Let's count 'em."

We threw them in the boat as we took them out of the net. Andrew's count was 76; mine was 77—that made 153 in all. We picked out a few big ones, then scaled and gutted them. Then we took them back and threw them on the open fire. The scent of their cooking was glorious as the aroma floated on the crisp morning air.

For a while we didn't say much—any of us. We all looked at Jesus like little children look at their father who has just returned from a long trip. Yes, we were grown men, but we knew inside we were really like children in need of direction.

In a little while, hot fish and bread were ready. The residual gray of the morning sky reminded me of the gray I had felt on that odd Thursday night when Jesus was arrested. Some things between Jesus and me needed to be cleared up. The issue was my denial of Him. I needed to confess, but I didn't really want to talk about it.

The truth is that I had impulsively promised Jesus—on that fateful Thursday—something I had failed to deliver: my loyalty. When Jesus really needed me, I wasn't there for him. I melted before the first accusation of a little girl who told some people that I was Jesus' friend. I lied my way out of my friendship with Jesus just to save my own skin. While I had no desire to confess my treachery to Him, I wanted to return to the joy of the relationship I had with Him.

The fish tasted good!

"Simon, son of John," said Jesus. "Do you love Me more than these?"

Jesus gestured toward the fish as he spoke. I knew what He meant. He had called me away from the sea and here I was back again. He called me to fish for men and here I was back fishing for fish. It was a fair question. *Did I love Jesus more than fishing?*

He was staring so directly at me that I felt very uncomfortable. I was too proud to repent publicly. Trying to avoid Jesus' directness, I crammed my mouth full of leftover fish and pretended I could avoid His question.

"Yes, Lord. You know I love You," I replied, mumbling with my mouth full of fish.

"Well then, feed My lambs."

I might have looked stupid to the others, but I was smart enough to know what He was saying. He had clearly called me into the care of sheep—the shepherding of others. Yet when Jesus had withheld Himself even for a little while, I became impatient and refused to wait on Him. I had left the calling I knew He had given me and was right back where He found me in the first place—Galilee. And Galilee lost its beauty with my failure to be obedient.

"Simon, son of John, do you truly love Me more than these?" Again Jesus gestured toward the fish when He said *these*.

Why did He ask me the same question again? Maybe He thought I hadn't paid attention the first time. I tried to act nonchalant by cramming another mouthful of fish in my face.

"Yes, Lord. You know that I love You," I said mumbling through the mouthful of food. "Sure is good fish, isn't it Andrew? Andrew?" Andrew wasn't listening to me.

A long period of silence followed. We all ate a little more.

"Simon, son of John, do you really love Me?" It was the third time He asked me that question. In the distant morning I heard a rooster crow. I stopped eating and swallowed the last bit of fish. It nearly choked me.

I swallowed hard.

I could not flip out another hurried answer. Jesus had asked me three times. Three times! Three . . . three . . . . "I tell you I don't know the man," I had spat out in blue-white profanity.

What the others heard Jesus asking me was not at all what I heard. I heard His deeper questions being leveled at my heart. "Peter why are you always promising so much more than you ever deliver? You denied Me when I hadn't a friend in the world. You said you'd stick with Me to prison and to death. If you meant it, why was there not another cross on that hill outside Jerusalem? One for you. Why just one for Me? Peter, do you love Me, or do you love fishing?"

Tears welled up in my eyes. I fell down before Jesus weeping. I held to him, "Yes Lord, You know everything; You know I love You."

"Then feed my sheep."

I knew what He was saying. "Peter, if you love Me, act like it. When you make a promise, stick to it no matter what it costs."

The others had grown very quiet. They listened intently as Jesus spoke. "I tell you the truth. When you were younger, you dressed yourself and went where you wanted; but when you are old you will stretch out your hands."

Jesus paused as He said those words, holding out His arms in the shape of a cross. All of our eyes fell on the scars in His hands. The ugly torn flesh around His wrists sent a chill through my frame. I shuddered, for I fully understood what He was saying. I wished He had been looking at someone else when He said it, but He was looking straight at me. I would die.

"Yes, you will stretch out your hands and someone else will dress you and lead you where you don't want to go. Follow Me, regardless."

I was washed by a new freedom. In one moment Jesus had let me know I would never be able to die for Him until I was committed to live for Him. Fishing was over. Shepherding had begun.

I needed some time to think.

I rose and walked away from the group. I passed my old boat now full of fishes. I walked along the seaside kicking up gravel with the soles of my sandals. A brisk wind began to blow. The sails of my little boat billowed outward in the new breeze.

Wind—I loved it! When it blew, my boat moved, when it did not blow, I rowed. Wind has always been God's benediction on sailors. Only the wind made the seas passable.

I knew out there somewhere God's wind would blow on my new

calling just as this wind had once compelled my tiny craft across Galilee. I had one of those wonderful flashbacks. Just a week or so before my last fishing trip I had been with Jesus where we had gathered ourselves together in a locked room for fear of the Jewish officials. As was His custom, Jesus just suddenly appeared in our midst. "Peace be unto you. As the Father has sent Me, I am sending you."

Then Jesus did a wonderful thing. He breathed on us and said, "Receive the Holy Spirit." His breath seemed at once a raging gale. It tore its way into our hearts.

Now as I walked alone by Galilee the wind stiffened to a gale. I had long felt the sea breezes also on my life, but this morning things were different. Now wind was more than moving air. Now wind was a promise, a symbol. Something was about to be born upon the earth. Fire like John the Baptist had preached about, was moving like judgment, like a purging flame of new joy. This flame would sear the open wounds of immorality into everlasting righteousness.

This fire of apocalypse would be driven by a divine Wind.

I knew I would someday stand—in a time not too far away—and bear witness to Jesus. This Wind would blow and the world would rejoice that at long last the universe made sense. I knew then that Jesus would ascend to His eternal throne, and those of us He left behind would wait for the Wind.

I stopped. I turned and looked back far down the beach. I saw a cluster of friends gathered around Jesus. Oh what He required! It was glorious and laborious, full of joy, yet requiring our very lives. I turned my eyes from the little group who hadn't yet suspected that they were world-changers. My eyes beheld a growing range of boiling thunderheads, driven by a strange and powerful storm. This wind would soon be loosed upon the world, and the world would glory in its breath.

This day for me was the first day of His eternity. All that we needed to change our dying world into the paradise of God was Wind. I felt the breeze grow firm and knew the promise would not long withhold itself.

> Come Wind.
> Replace this small frail breeze.
> Blow healing, saving grace from sea to sea,
> > till every wound is seared so splendidly
> > that every ocean envies Galilee.

I Am Sending You

It is a rare morning when most Americans do not think their alarm clocks are ringing too early! According to many health authorities, we live in a nation of sleep-deprived adults. Many of us try to do too much, do it until too late at night, and, consequently, begin the next day without enough sleep. Regardless of how much sleep we have had, it appears we sleepers have at least three options when we hear the ringing or buzzing of our alarm clocks. Our first option is to think, *I'm glad to know what time it is, but I'm going to turn off this terrible buzzing noise and go back to sleep!* —and to do just that! The second option is to press the snooze bar, thinking, *I'll do something soon about getting up and starting my day...but, not now...not yet.* The third option (and usually the best option) is to get up and act NOW.

Whenever we are faced with challenges in our walk with Christ, we have the same three options. We can think to ourselves, *I'm glad I've been made aware of this challenge, but I am going to stay the way I was before hearing it!* Our second option is one of good intentions: *I have heard the challenge and I will do something soon, but, not right now...not yet.* The third (and again the best option) is to hear the challenge and act NOW.

These same three options are ours now that we've considered the four basic aspects of this study: Christ's invitation, *Follow Me*; the need for the power and presence of God found through prayer; the importance of serving fellow believers; and the command to love and meet the needs of our neighbors. Now—will you go back to a state of spiritual sleep? Will you commit to doing something about what you have learned, but put it off until later? Or will you get up and act NOW on what God has shown you?

Just as the wearing of a camp T-shirt is not the best way to recognize that a teenager has spent a week studying the Bible at youth camp, a dog-eared and written-in copy of *The J Files* is not the best way for others to recognize your involvement in a study of following the example of the life of Christ! Instead, there are four basic ways in which others will be able to see a new commitment to following Christ's example.

1. Walk as Jesus walked.—We are to go the places Jesus would go if He lived in our cities. After reviewing the places Jesus went to meet needs, we must show new commitment by going places to which we've not gone in the past.

2. See as Jesus saw.—We are to notice needs in a clearer way than we noticed them in the past. Jesus' example is clear: No longer do we have the option of walking past needs and forgetting them.

3. Speak as Jesus spoke.—We are given the authority to minister in His name, speaking His truths to all who need to hear them. He offers new life to people today, just as He offered it to the Samaritan woman at the well. We must tell others about the peace of which He speaks.

4. Love as Jesus loved.—Jesus showed clearly that love is given without consideration of the merit of the individual. How can we love in this way? We must make our love something we do, not something we merely discuss.

If we consistently walk as He walked, see as He saw, speak as He spoke, and love as He loved, we will discover and meet needs of those He would touch if He were physically with us here on earth.

Consider which of the four evidences of a new commitment least characterizes you. In the space below each evidence, list anything you must do or any changes you must make in order to follow Christ's example in this area.

1. Going the places Jesus would go

2. Opening your eyes to see needs as Jesus saw them

3. Speaking the words to those who need to hear them

4. Loving in the unconditional way Jesus loved

In the last days of Christ on earth before His ascension to heaven, the disciples, too, were faced with a new challenge—to continue the mission of Christ without His physical presence. This story begins in John 20:19 as the disciples were hidden behind locked doors. Jesus appeared to them, showing His wounded hands and side. He commissioned the disciples to the task of taking His message to others because He would no longer be a physical, bodily presence in the world. Jesus' words commission us, as well: *As the Father has sent me, I am sending you.* He then breathed the Holy Spirit into their lives to give them the power to carry out the task.

Beginning in John 21:15 we are told of a conversation between Simon Peter and Christ after eating a meal of fish they had caught earlier that day. Jesus asked Peter three times, *Simon, son of John, do you love me?* Jesus did not use the same form of the Greek word for *love* in each of the three questions. He used the word *agapao* in the first two questions, asking if Peter had a high, spiritual, self-sacrificing devotion to Him. In his replies Peter chose the word *phileo*, meaning "brotherly love" and "affection." The first time Christ asked Peter the question, *Do you love me?* He added the phrase *more than these*. He may have been asking if Peter loved Him more than the boats and nets he used while fishing. Or, Christ could have been asking if Peter loved Him more than the other disciples sitting around the fire where they had cooked the meal. Most likely, Jesus was asking Peter if he loved Him more than all the broken vows of Peter's past. The third time Jesus asked Peter, *Do you love me?* He used the same word, *phileo*, that Peter had used in his answers, instead of His earlier choice of the higher love, *agapao*.

Christ was, in essence, asking Peter, "Do you even love me in the manner of friendship and affectionate brotherly love?" Peter's reply, again, was *You know that I love (phileo) you*, preceded by the statement, *Lord, you know all things*. This third question must have brought back to Peter's mind his three denials of Christ before the crucifixion. Sadly, Peter was unable to state his love for Christ in the superior, or *agape* form of love.

Interwoven throughout these questions and answers, Christ issued the commands, "Feed my lambs and take care of my sheep." He used different Greek words as He gave these instructions. One word translated *feed* means to furnish nutrients for the flock. Another means to provide care, guidance, and protection for the flock. It appears Christ was instructing Peter to provide both food and protection for believers, both the mature (sheep) and the young (lambs). This commission is ours, also.

As we consider the commissions given by our risen Christ, the Great Commission comes to the forefront of our thoughts. Recorded in Matthew 28:18-20, these were Christ's last words before He ascended to heaven to the Father:

> *All authority in heaven and on earth has been given to me. Therefore go and make disciples of all nations, baptizing them in the name of the Father and of the Son and of the Holy Spirit, and teaching them to obey everything I have commanded you. And surely I am with you always, to the very end of the age.*

Jesus began with a statement of the power and authority that had been given to Him. He then instructed His disciples to go and make disciples—the idea being to bring others under Christ's teaching and rule as we go. This should be a natural way of life for us as believers—we are to teach all nations, not just those of our particular race or nationality. We are to teach obedience to the things Jesus commanded while He was on the earth. Jesus then promised the disciples He would be with them—and all believers—always. This Great Commission applies to all Christians. We must take very seriously our Lord's command to go, make disciples, baptize, and teach. We must not only win people but train them to do all that Christ commands.

This commission is also expressed by Paul. Paul realized he was Christ's appointed representative to take His message to others, as are all believers. He encouraged his readers to understand that their responsibility had only begun when they accepted the grace of Christ. It was then their task to pass it on to others.

When you are not acting upon the commission of Christ, it is natural to assume you may not consider it a commission intended for you. If you believe the words of Jesus in Matthew 28:18-20, as well as the other expressions of that commission in Scripture are your commission, complete the following statements.

I believe Jesus commissioned me to preach the Gospel and seek to lead others to Him. This week I will show this belief by:

I believe Jesus commissioned me to make disciples, teaching obedience to His commandments. This week I will show this belief by:

Helping people learn how to be like Christ in order to fulfill their mission for Christ is one of the major reasons churches provide Bible study groups. If you teach or hold a leadership position in a Bible study class, you must determine how well your class is preparing people each week for being on mission for God. The prayer, Bible study, fellowship, and ministry of the class should be focused in that direction. The class also becomes one of the main arenas in which new people, touched by the daily interactions of God's people on mission, are introduced to Christ. In short, a youth Bible study class is a small community of teenagers on mission for God, reaching out and incorporating new youth into that community. How well does your class measure up?

Before going farther, complete the "Class Mission" worksheet on page 94.

Lead your class to calculate its networking potential. Simply ask each member to list the number of people they have some contact with each working day through conversation, telephone, computer, or business transaction. Add their totals together and multiply by the days of the week. When your class meets each week, consider how much impact participants can have during the coming week. Guide members to participate in their networks of contact the way Christ would were He in their shoes.

> Pause here and calculate your own network potential.
>
> ## Your Network Potential
>
> Calculating your network potential: Take a typical day of your week, then estimate the number of people with whom you had some kind of contact that day.
>
> Family members _____
> People at work and/or school _____
> People talked to on the phone or by computer _____
> People met casually (gas station, grocery, and so forth) _____
> People met during recreational activities _____
> Others _____
> TOTAL _____
>
> Multiply your total for one day times five (typical school or work week):
> Your weekly networking potential _____

One of the ways we can carry out the Great Commission is through a process known to Christians as "discipling." In the secular world a similar relationship, known as "mentoring," is a very popular concept. The relationship of discipling or mentoring involves someone who undertakes the training or tutoring of a person who may not have the experience or expertise of the trainer or tutor. The relationship involves teaching, leading by example, and encouragement.

As a youth minister, it has been my privilege to become acquainted with others either studying youth ministry or already active in it. Because I had more experience, I tried to teach them what I knew. I sought to lead by example and encourage them in the difficult aspects of ministering to teenagers. Now, many years later, they are firmly established in the field of youth ministry and are serving their local churches in an excellent way. What a thrill it is for me to watch as they, too, mentor young people in youth ministry!

Think of someone who has successfully taught you, trained you, or led you in the Christian life or in some other area of your life. In the space below, list that person's character qualities and a few of the ways he or she encouraged, taught, and trained you.

Jesus provided the clearest example of discipling in his relationship with the twelve men who followed Him in His earthly ministry. These disciples were to announce the good news of the Kingdom of Christ. The term *disciple* comes from a Latin root meaning *learner* or *pupil*. In the Greek language *disciple* referred to an adherent of a particular teacher or religious/philosophical school. This individual was to learn, study, and pass along the teachings of the Master.

Dr. J.M. Price, founder of the School of Religious Education at Southwestern Baptist Theological Seminary, wrote an excellent book, *Jesus, the Teacher*, published in 1946.[1] In this short work, he examined various aspects of Jesus' teaching and training of individuals. Dr. Price suggested six qualifications that made Jesus perfectly fitted for such a task. We can apply these same six qualifications to those who want to enter a relationship of mentoring or discipling others.

    1. Jesus embodied the truth.—His most effective message was Himself and the example He set in each and every situation. As Dr. Price wrote, the best binding for the Gospels is not Moroccan leather, but human skin!

    2. Jesus desired to serve. Jesus was interested in people and wanted to help them. He was never too proud, too tired, or too busy to serve others.

    3. Jesus believed in teaching. He saw teaching as a primary way in which He could shape the attitudes and behavior of people. He did not have the professional credentials of a scribe or a rabbi, but teaching was His way of life.

4. Jesus knew the Scriptures, His main textbook. He used Scripture on many occasions, one example being His conversation with His disciples who did not recognize Him as they walked on the road to Emmaus.

5. Jesus understood human nature. Teaching and leading others depends upon an understanding of people and the way they act and think. He understood the needs of those with whom He came in contact.

6. Jesus mastered the art. He probably did not study teaching methods and procedures. Yet, He grasped the art of teaching and was a master teacher. He used all of the teaching-learning methods that are taught today.

Which of these six qualifications is your strongest qualification for teaching and training others? In which area do you need the most work? Write your answers to both questions in the space below.

The apostle Paul also provides an excellent example of discipling or mentoring another individual. After a difficult experience with John Mark, Paul began a mentoring-type relationship with Timothy. Timothy was like a son to Paul, for he became a Christian after Paul's first missionary journey to Lystra. Paul described him as his true son in the faith. Their relationship is considered a classic model of the teacher/learner or mentor/protégé relationship. Paul demonstrated principles of mentoring through the following characteristics of his relationship with Timothy and others whom he led to grow in Christian maturity.

1. Paul encouraged Timothy. He reminded him of his heritage of faith from his grandmother Lois and his mother Eunice.

2. Paul prayed for Timothy. We are reminded of these prayers in 2 Timothy 1:3 when Paul wrote *I thank God...as night and day I constantly remember you in my prayers.*

3. Paul considered Timothy a co-worker. He did not relegate him to a subservient position.

4. Paul provided doctrinal instruction for Timothy. One example of such instruction is found in 2 Timothy 3:16 as Paul listed characteristics of the Scriptures. He also taught of the role of deacons and church officers.

5. Paul sought to prepare Timothy for situations he would face. Because Timothy was half Jewish, half Greek, Paul encouraged him to be circumcised in order to be better received by the Jewish believers he would seek to win to Christ.

6. Paul advised Timothy concerning personal behavior. In 1 Timothy 6:20 he warned Timothy to stay away from idle talk (*turn away from godless chatter*), and he reminded him of the ways a young man's behavior could serve as an example for other believers—*Don't let anyone look down on you because you are young, but set an example for the believers in speech, in life, in love, in faith and in purity.*

7. Paul allowed Timothy to gain experience in working without him. He

sent Timothy to minister as his representative in Corinth, in Thessalonica, and in Ephesus. He wanted Timothy to learn to work on his own.

8. Paul trusted Timothy's judgment. He had not planned to make a return visit to the Corinthian church, but did so after hearing Timothy's report of crisis in the church.

9. Paul showed great respect for Timothy and affirmed this respect before others. In Philippians 2:19-22, Paul paid Timothy a tremendous compliment as he described him as *the only one who takes a genuine interest in your welfare, stating that he has proved himself, because as a son with his father he has served with me in the work of the gospel*. He also described Timothy as *a faithful follower of Christ who would remind you of my way of life in Christ Jesus*.

10. Paul was always willing to lead by example. He boldly invited others to view his life carefully.

11. Paul pointed others to the highest goal. He wrote: *I press on toward the goal to win the prize for which God has called me heavenward in Christ Jesus*.

12. Paul challenged Timothy to share what he learned with others. In 2 Timothy 2:2 Paul wrote: *And the things you have heard me say in the presence of many witnesses entrust to reliable men who will also be qualified to teach others*. This is often referred to as the "principle of multiplication." Instead of adding new believers one by one, with no training for them in how to win others, we win new converts and take the time to train them to grow in Christ and win others. This process may take longer at first, but it is more productive, for it results in many more people who are working and adding others to the Kingdom.

As we consider the challenge of mentoring or discipling others in the Christian life, we must try to manifest these same qualities of Paul's mentoring relationships. What are some situations in which mentoring would be a desirable option for getting others involved with the ultimate goal of Christian growth? Listed below are a few possibilities.

1. Witnessing and visitation
2. Teaching Sunday School or teaching in another program organization of the church
3. Working in mission activities, such as soup kitchens, clothes closets and food pantries
4. Accepting committee responsibilities in the church, which may be as varied as enlisting Sunday School workers, making preparations for the Lord's Supper or baptism, or planning church-wide events.
5. Relation-based mentoring, such as older men sharing their wisdom and experience with younger men, husbands and fathers; older women sharing with younger women, wives, and mothers.
6. Teenagers adopting a "little brother" or "little sister" from among the younger middle schoolers or older children in the church for discipleship and friendship.
7. All ages establishing discipleship pairings which major in the basic growth disciplines of the Christian life.

In the space below, list your areas of interest and/or experience, both in the church and in other areas of your life. Choose one or two areas in which you would consider serving as a mentor to a younger or less experienced person. Beside each area, write a few ideas concerning the types of information and experience you would like to pass on to that person.

There are various ways to develop a mentoring ministry. Consider the following basic guidelines and modify them to fit the situation within your church.

1. Make a commitment to mentor an individual for a period of at least six months.
2. Discover persons who would benefit from being involved in this type of relationship. Include those who are inactive in the life of your church as well as those who are already actively involved.
3. Provide opportunities for these persons to become aware of the subject areas in which mentoring is offered.
4. Provide opportunities for these persons to assess their gifts, abilities, and interests.
5. Develop an intentional strategy for mentoring, such as meeting together, building relationships, praying together, and working together over a specified period of time.
6. Work toward the goal of the person being mentored working independently.
7. Work toward readying the person mentored to become a mentor or assist another mentor after a minimum of six months' experience.
8. Ensure a time of evaluation during which the mentor and the one mentored can share ideas and suggestions in order to strengthen the procedures of the mentoring ministry.

Paul provided a statement of philosophy for one who is willing to make the investment of being a mentor in another person's life. He wrote describing the relationship of himself, Silvanus (Silas), and Timothy with the Thessalonian believers. They held nothing back in their ministry to the Thessalonians. This is a model for our love relationship with those we wish to encourage in Christian growth.

You may have already begun to think of a person or persons you would be interested in mentoring. Write their initials in the space below, asking God to lead you as you consider these important relationships.

The emphasis given to discipling and mentoring is significant because of the role these actions can play in the mission of the church. Jesus sought to lead His disciples into an awareness of their responsibility in building and passing on a mission movement. The term *mission* is not found in the Bible, yet the concept permeates Scripture. As believers, we are to go to the people; not wait for them to come to us. We are to nurture and nourish young believers to share their faith with others. Jesus did not give the Great Commission as an afterthought, but as the focus of His instruction to the church. He was sent from the Father to preach, teach, heal, serve, and die for others. As God sent Christ, Christ sends us. We have been given the power and authority to reach others for Him.

John 15:1-17 provides a synopsis of our study of following the example of Christ. All four of the aspects we have studied are included. This Scripture passage is a beautiful picture of the believer (the branch) who is in union with Christ (the Vine), the relationship which occurs when we say *yes* to Christ's invitation, *Follow Me*! God the Father is the husbandman, or the one who cares for the Vine. The intention of the relationship between the Vine and the branches is to bear more fruit. It is in this relationship that we experience a prayer life that is productive and purposeful, for our wills are abiding in His. Fruit-bearing is impossible unless a believer remains connected to the Vine. If a branch doesn't bear fruit, it is removed. If a branch bears fruit, it is pruned, or cleansed, so that it may bear more fruit. One of the ways we bear fruit is in obedience to His command to love each other as He has loved us. This includes both those in the family of faith and our neighbors whom we may not even know. God may choose to remove whatever stands in the way of our usefulness to Him, regardless of how painful an experience it is.

Abiding in the Vine is both a privilege and a responsibility . The responsibility lies in keeping His commandments. The privilege is the joy we know in this kind of relationship with Christ. Jesus chose to love us and give His life for us. He stated His intention for us to bear fruit in the lives of others that would last for eternity. When we are about this business of Christ, He will supply everything we need. If we willingly accept the challenge of following His example in a life of discipleship, prayer, serving fellow believers, and loving our neighbors, He is ready to provide the necessary nourishment and power. The Father will be glorified when we bear much fruit, showing ourselves to be disciples of His Son.

What have you gained from this study? What were your levels of awareness and commitment when you began the study? Listed below are the four chapter topics and a rating scale. Place a *check* in the space before the phrase that best describes your attitude when beginning this study. Place an *x* in the space before the phrase that best describes your attitude now.

Following Christ
___I have a low level of awareness and/or interest in this topic.
___I have a basic knowledge of this topic.
___I am considering deeper involvement in this area.
___I have a special interest in this topic.
___I have made a commitment to more completely follow Christ's call to
    discipleship in every area of my life.
___I am considering becoming a mentor to another person in the area of
   Christ's call to discipleship.

Prayer
___I have a low level of awareness and/or interest in this topic.
___I have a basic knowledge of this topic.
___I am considering deeper involvement in this area.
___I have a special interest in this topic.
___I have made a commitment to deepen my walk with Christ through
   more consistent fellowship with Him in prayer
___I am considering becoming a mentor to another person in the area of
   deepening one's prayer life.

Loving and Serving Other Believers
___I have a low level of awareness and/or interest in this topic.
___I have a basic knowledge of this topic.
___I am considering deeper involvement in this area.
___I have a special interest in this topic.
___I have made a commitment to adopt a servant's attitude among my fellow believers, looking for ways to love and serve those in the household of faith.
___I am considering becoming a mentor to another person in the area of loving and serving other believers.

Loving One's Neighbor
___I have a low level of awareness and/or interest in this topic.
___I have a basic knowledge of this topic.
___I am considering deeper involvement in this area.
___I have a special interest in this topic.
___I have made a commitment to reach out to people in need of any type of help.
___I am considering becoming a mentor to another person in the area of meeting the needs of our "neighbor."

When Christ asked Peter three times, "Do you love me?" He was asking for a statement of Peter's level of commitment. Peter, for whatever reason, chose to indicate a different level of love than that for which Christ was asking. Christ asks us, also, for an indication of our level of commitment. Whenever Christ confronts us with His truth, He gives us the opportunity to respond. Today, He continues to ask:
Do you love (agape) me? What is your answer?

At the close of each chapter you were given the opportunity to complete a "stretching" exercise. The purpose of these activities is to encourage us to stretch our attitudes, our commitments, and our willingness to follow the example Christ set for us when He lived on earth. Take a few minutes to review your responses to those stretching exercises by looking back at the responses you made. Do you still feel the same way? Are you ready to make a deeper commitment in at least one of the areas we've studied? Are you ready to plug into the power source—to abide in Christ—in order to follow His will?

Write a prayer of commitment to God, asking for His help in fulfilling your commitment. Acknowledge any fears and insecurities you might have, asking for His peace and power as you carry out your commitment.

[1]. Dr. J.M. Price, *Jesus, The Teacher* (Nashville: Convention Press, 1946), 1-13.

A study of *Jesus on Leadership: Becoming a Servant Leader* (7700-72) is a powerful next step for growing disciples. Following Christ's example leads to a path of servanthood. It is the model that rejects the world's view of leadership and adopts Christ's example. Jesus taught that leaders are those persons who serve for His glory, not for their gain. In too many churches today, head tables have replaced the towel and washbasin as symbols of leadership among God's people. The resource *Jesus on Leadership* can lead members of the body of Christ to apply biblical principles of servant leadership to all areas of their ministries. This five-week interactive workbook can develop leaders in your church who follow His example and mandate to do kingdom work.

Class Mission

How well is our class doing in fulfilling its mission? Rate your class on the basis of *1* being low and *5* being high.

1. We have a sense of being on mission.	1 2 3 4 5
2. We can easily state our mission to each other.	1 2 3 4 5
3. We understand where our mission field begins.	1 2 3 4 5
4. We share and report our experiences as missionaries.	1 2 3 4 5
5. We pray for each other concerning our mission roles.	1 2 3 4 5
6. We study the Bible each week to help us be missionaries.	1 2 3 4 5
7. We gladly bring friends and acquaintances to Bible study.	1 2 3 4 5
8. We talk openly about what it means to follow Christ.	1 2 3 4 5
9. We enjoy fellowship with each other and with new people.	1 2 3 4 5
10. We admit to each other our fears and failures on mission.	1 2 3 4 5
11. We pray for people in need.	1 2 3 4 5
12. We work together to help people in need.	1 2 3 4 5
13. We work together to talk with people about Jesus.	1 2 3 4 5
14. We bring our offerings to provide money for missions.	1 2 3 4 5
15. We participate in church mission projects.	1 2 3 4 5

My Covenant as a follower of Christ's example

In the space below write out your covenant with God to follow Christ's example by going where Christ would go, loving those whom Christ would love, doing what Christ would do, and teaching what Christ would teach.

_____

_____

_____

_____

_____

_____

_____

_____

_____

Signed: _____

CHRISTIAN GROWTH STUDY PLAN
Preparing Christians to Serve

In the **Christian Growth Study Plan (formerly Church Study Course)**, this book *The J Files, Follow Christ's Example: Youth* is a resource for course credit in three Leadership and Skill Development diploma plans. To receive credit, read the book, complete the learning activities, show your work to your pastor, a staff member or church leader, then complete the following information. This page may be duplicated. Send the completed page to:

**Christian Growth Study Plan
127 Ninth Avenue, North, MSN 117
Nashville, TN 37234-0117
FAX: (615)251-5067**

For information about the Christian Growth Study Plan, refer to the current Christian Growth Study Plan Catalog. Your church office may have a copy. If not, request a free copy from the Christian Growth Study Plan office (615/251-2525).

COURSE CREDIT INFORMATION

Please check the appropriate box indicating the diploma you want to apply this credit. You may check more than one.

- ❏ **Youth Leadership—Sunday School Ministry (LS-0028)**
- ❏ **Reaching People Through Bible Study Projects and Groups (LS-0051)**
- ❏ **Special Education in Sunday School (LS-0107)**

PARTICIPANT INFORMATION

Social Security Number | Personal CGSP Number* | Date of Birth

Name (First, MI, Last)
❏ Mr. ❏ Miss
❏ Mrs. ❏

Home Phone

Address (Street, Route, or P.O. Box) | City, State | Zip Code

CHURCH INFORMATION

Church Name

Address (Street, Route, or P.O. Box) | City, State | Zip Code

CHANGE REQUEST ONLY

❏ Former Name

❏ Former Address | City, State | Zip Code

❏ Former Church | City, State | Zip Code

Signature of Pastor, Conference Leader, or Other Church Leader | Date

*New participants are requested but not required to give SS# and date of birth. Existing participants, please give CGSP# when using SS# for the first time. Thereafter, only one ID# is required. *Mail To:* Christian Growth Study Plan, 127 Ninth Ave., North, MSN 117, Nashville, TN 37234-0117. Fax: (615)251-5067